Mousetracks
A Kid's Computer Idea Book

Peggy Steinhauser

TRICYCLE PRESS
Berkeley, California

Acknowledgments

Congratulations to parents and teachers who recognize that children can and should use the computer to create rewarding projects of their own. Seeing the excitement and sense of accomplishment on the faces of my students was the true inspiration for this book. I am very happy to be working with Alan Kellock, whose belief in this project helped bring it to fruition. Thanks to Kevin Tseng for his technical support, and to inspirations and friends like Blanche Braillard, Shelley VanClief, Nancy Layton, my mom, and my husband, Greg. Thank you to my brilliant lifelong students: Catherine, Jennifer, and Claire. I'm also sending e-mail to heaven to thank my big dog, Jake, who slept quietly under my computer every night while I created this book.

Copyright © 1997 by Peggy Steinhauser

TRICYCLE PRESS
P.O. Box 7123
Berkeley, California 94707

Cover design by Cale Burr and Toni Tajima
Text design by Toni Tajima

Library of Congress Cataloging-in-Publication Data
Steinhauser, Peggy, 1957–
   Mousetracks: a kid's computer idea book/Peggy Steinhauser.
     p. cm.
   Includes indexes.
   Summary: Helps the reader learn how to use computer graphics and word processing programs while working on projects on a variety of topics.
   ISNBN 1–883672–48–1
   1. Microcomputers—Juvenile literature. [1. Computer graphics. 2. Word processing. 3. Microcomputers.] I. Title.
   QA76.23.S74 1997
   004.16—dc20   96-29330
                                      CIP
                                      AC

First Tricycle Press printing, 1997
Printed in Hong Kong
2 3 4 5 6 7 — 01 00 99 98 97

CONTENTS

A MESSAGE TO PARENTS AND EDUCATORS

Mousetracks offers more than 70 innovative and fun projects for kids ages 5 to 10 to do on a computer. Unlike most computer games and other forms of "edutainment," *Mousetracks* projects combine technical learning with imagination, and provide satisfying, printed results. A basic drawing program, word processing software, and a printer are all that you need to get started. *Mousetracks* projects have been designed for kids to meet these goals:

• To learn to use the computer as a tool

The activities in *Mousetracks* introduce tools, one by one, that are part of each graphic or word processing program. As the activities progress, the tools and skills build on one another. These skills are age appropriate; the early activities rely on graphic programs, while later ones bring in word processing. By the end of the book, kids will be able to promote their love and knowledge of sports, space flight, or ancient Egypt; write and illustrate their own newspaper and comics; and even think about the ways a computer helps in business.

• To produce a useful, lasting result

Kids can use *Mousetracks* projects to produce cards, gifts, school work, party decorations, trading cards, and many, many more printed pieces. Printing a project to show to family, friends, and teachers, provides a tremendous feeling of accomplishment and satisfaction in kids.

• To have fun

Rainforests, dinosaurs, and sports are just a few of the many kid-pleasing topics in *Mousetracks*. Plus, clear, step-by-step instructions and samples of finished projects will encourage kids to jump right in and get started. Projects are sure to be fun—they have been rigorously kid-tested at Mousetrap Computer Workshop, Inc., an after-school center offering computer enrichment classes.

A MESSAGE TO KIDS

Are you ready for this computer challenge? Get ready to show off the computer tools you know, find out new ways to use those tools, and even learn some new ones. The sample projects in this book are for you to try, but they're also there to give you ideas for your own creations. There are lots of reasons to use a computer to draw and write. Drawing with computer tools is easy. You can make perfect circles and squares, straight lines, and use tons of colors. Writing is pretty simple, too. Just click on the letter tool, and use the keyboard. The more you do it, the faster you get. Printing is the best. You can make as many copies as you want, and keep them in a scrapbook, put them on your wall, or take them to school. (Who knows, maybe you'll get extra credit!)

Here are a few important things to know before you start:

* Each project has a list of instructions. The first thing to do is to go to your drawing or word processing program. After you do that, start at instruction number 1, and keep going until you are happy with the project.

* The examples in this book show you just one way to do the project. Everyone's project will look a little different.

* You print each project when you're finished. You can decide which ones you want to save as files on the computer. If the instructions tell you to save, please do so because you will need to open that file again later.

* Plain white paper can be used to print most projects, but some projects include other printing ideas, like card stock, transparencies, and label sheets. Ask an adult if your printer can handle these other papers before you buy and try them!

* Keep your projects and show them off. Cover them with report covers, put them in a notebook, hang them up, or think of your own way.

* Please read the Tech Talk and Tool Talk sections with an adult before you start.

TECH TALK

Graphic projects in this book can be done in Kid Pix, Kid Works 2, Paintbrush in Windows, Fine Artist, Flying Colors, or any number of other graphic programs. Word processing projects in this book can be done in Children's Writing and Publishing Center, Creative Writer, WordPerfect, Microsoft Word, or just about any other word processing program.

You will need a color monitor for most of these activities. You should use a color printer, but if you don't have one you can do the projects in color on screen, print them in black and white, and color the printouts with markers, crayons, or pencils. For some projects you'll need to look things up in an encyclopedia. Use a kids' CD-ROM encyclopedia if you have one, or you can dial into the reference area of an on-line service (ask an adult first!). Of course, a book will do just fine.

TOOL TALK

One thing most graphic and word processing programs have in common is a blank screen and tools. The tools in different programs may have different names and different symbols, but they usually do the same thing. In this book, one name is used for each tool. The tool name used is the one closest to what exactly the tool does or what the result looks like. For example, the circle tool creates a circle, the spray can tool makes a mark on the page that resembles spray paint, and the letter tool writes letters. So don't worry if the directions tell you to grab the crackle tool and you don't have one. Just check this Tool Talk section and look for a tool that makes a crooked line. You may want to practice with each tool before you start a *Mousetracks* project.

Projects in this book use the keyboard and the mouse. The names of keyboard keys to use (like Enter and Tab) will always start with a capital letter. Keep reading to find out more.

Terms to Know

Click: To press the mouse button, then release it quickly.

Cursor: The blinking line on your computer screen. The place the mouse is resting before you type a word.

Drag: To click on something and move it to a new place while holding down the mouse button.

File: Anything that you draw or write on the computer and save with its own name.

Font: The different kinds of letters that you can make with your letter, word, or typewriter tools.

Import: To put a file you've made another time into the file you are working on now.

Justification: To "justify" means to line up evenly. If you right justify a sentence, the sentence moves to the right side of your page. If you left justify, it moves to the left. The same goes for center. Full justification stretches out your words so that they line up on both sides of the page.

Mouse: The computer tool you hold in your hand. It tells your computer what you want to do. On screen, it shows up as an arrow or a blinking line (cursor).

Save: To keep a file that you create on the computer so that it can be opened again. To save a file, you must also give it its own name.

Save As: Another way of saving a file, which means giving an old file a new name without erasing the old file.

Stamp: One of the drawing tools that lets you choose pictures and put them on your computer page.

Keyboard keys to know:

Backspace: Erases something while moving backward.

Command: Same as Control.

Control (ctrl): When combined with other keys, this key will change the way something looks on screen. (In some drawing programs, it can make things larger.)

Delete: Erases something while moving forward, though on some computers this works like a Backspace key and erases things moving backward.

Enter/Return: Moves the cursor to the next line.

Escape (esc): Can help you quit a program, or sometimes it takes your computer back one screen.

Option: Same as Control.

Shift: Makes keyboard letters capital while you type them.

Space Bar: Moves the cursor one space forward.

Tab: Moves the cursor five spaces forward.

Up, Down, Left, Right arrows: Moves the cursor one space—or many spaces if you hold the key down—in any of these directions.

These are some of the drawing tools used in this book:

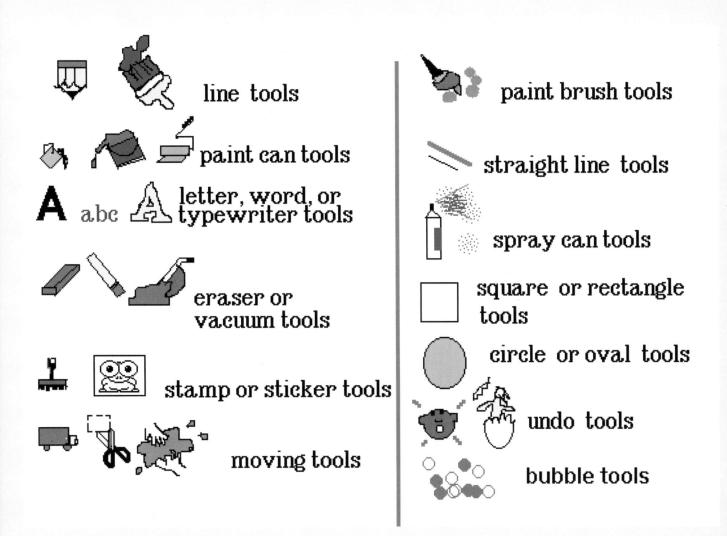

line tools

paint can tools

A abc letter, word, or typewriter tools

eraser or vacuum tools

stamp or sticker tools

moving tools

paint brush tools

straight line tools

spray can tools

square or rectangle tools

circle or oval tools

undo tools

bubble tools

These are some of the word processing commands you may need:

Example commands are shown in the two most commonly used word processing programs, WordPerfect (Wp) and Microsoft Word (W). If you are using a different word processing program, the command steps may be different. Don't worry—you can still end up with the same result. Your program may also include buttons as shortcuts for these commands.

TO HIGHLIGHT   To choose text with the mouse by clicking and holding, dragging, releasing; looks like this.

TOOLS	WHAT IT DOES	COMMANDS OR BUTTONS TO DO IT
CUT & PASTE	Moves text from one place to another	Highlight text, choose Edit, then choose Cut Place mouse, choose Edit, Paste (Wp & W)
CENTER	Puts text in the center of page	Highlight text, choose Format, choose Justification, choose Center (Wp) Highlight text, choose Format, choose Paragraph, and under Alignment choose Center (W)
CHANGE FONT	Changes letter sizes and styles	Highlight text, Format, Font, pick type style & size (Wp & W) 12 pt., 24 pt., 30 pt.
HORIZONTAL LINE	Makes a line across page	Choose Graphics, horizontal line (Wp) Choose Format, Borders & Shading (W)
COLUMNS	Makes columns	Choose Format, Columns, define 1 2 3 4 (Wp) Choose Format, columns 1 2 3 4 (W)
OPEN FILE	Opens a file	Choose File, highlight the one you want, click Open
SAVE FILE	Saves a file	Choose File, click Save, then type your file name
PRINT FILE	Prints a file	Choose File, click Print
IMPORT PICTURE	Brings a picture into your file	Choose Graphics, choose Image (Wp) Choose Insert, then Picture (W)
UNDO	Takes away the last move you did	Choose Edit, then Undo
TAB	Moves the cursor 5 spaces	Press Tab key (on the keyboard)
BULLETS	Puts marks in front of a list	Choose Insert, choose Bullets or Numbers (Wp) Choose Format, then Bullets & Numbering (W)
BORDER	Puts border around text	Highlight text, Format, Paragraph, Border (Wp) Highlight text, Format, Borders & Shading (W)

1 PLAY GAMES WITH COLORS AND PATTERNS

Practice making and mixing colors. Mix some colors and match some colors. Paint the colors of the rainbow. Use computer colors and tools to make patterns, or make patterns without any color at all. Use patterns to make some fun games to play with your friends.

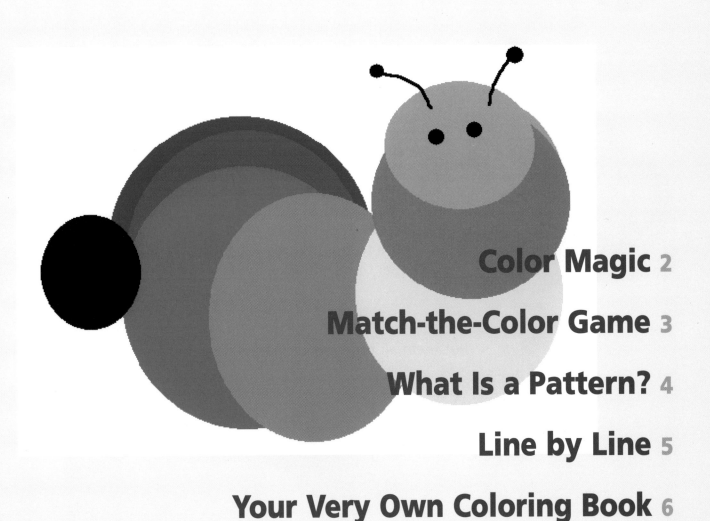

1

Color Magic

Most computers have lots of colors to paint with. But did you know that you can make your own colors on the computer? Is it magic? Not really. All you have to do is start with three colors. Those three colors are the primary colors red, yellow, and blue.

To make a picture with the primary colors in your drawing program—

1. Use your spray can tool with each of the 3 primary colors and spray a circle of color. Label them RED, YELLOW, BLUE.

2. Next, make more colors. Try to spray evenly—don't spray too much in one place. Making the colors just right might take a couple of tries. Between your red and blue circles start a new circle, using some red and some blue color. What color do you see now? Do you see purple? Take your time, you may need a lot of each color. Try mixing red and yellow. Do you see orange? The last mixture to try is blue and yellow to make green. Label these colors.

3. Use the spray can and all six colors to draw a rainbow. Put them all together to make this lovely arch of color!

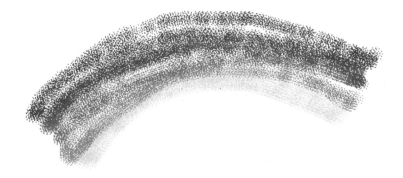

Match-the-Color Game

Play a game with colors. Make your game card and play the game
on the computer by yourself, or with a friend.

To make the game card in your drawing program—

1. Make 6 squares on the left side of your page with your square tool.

2. Pick 6 colors. Fill each square with one color using your paint can tool. Draw a line with your straight line tool across the page next to each square. You can make the line the same color as the square if you want to.

3. Check to see if your game card looks like this one.

Now play the game! Click your stamp tool and see how many stamps you can find that match the colors of your squares. If your stamp tools are in color, stamp on the line with the same color. If your stamps are not in color, stamp the picture next to the color that the stamp would be in real life. Then use your paint can tool to color the stamp. Keep stamping until one of the lines is full. That color is the winner. For the record, count the stamps on each line and stamp the number at the end of the line. Try the game again by taking turns with a friend.

This card is
ready to play!

Red won this
color matching game!

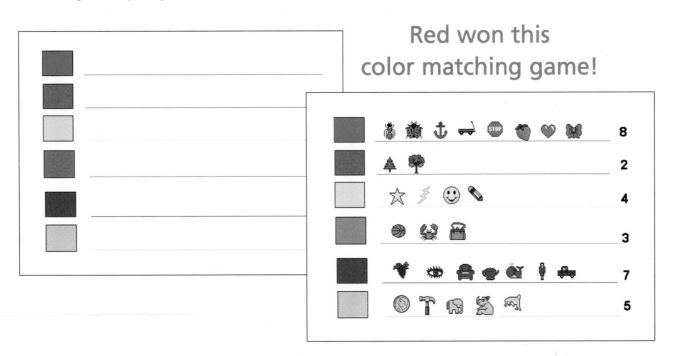

What Is a Pattern?

A pattern is the way colors, shapes, or lines are arranged or repeated in some order.

> ABC ABC ABC ABC
> is a pattern.
>
> *?*?*?*?*?*?*?*?
> is a pattern.

To make some patterns in your drawing program—

1. Click your stamp tool to stamp some of these patterns. When you get to the blank lines, fill in the patterns.

2. To make your own patterns, click your circle tool to draw circles the same size. *Hint: Start circles at the top left part of the circle, and pull the mouse pointer down and to the right.* Use the paint can tool to fill in the circles in a pattern.

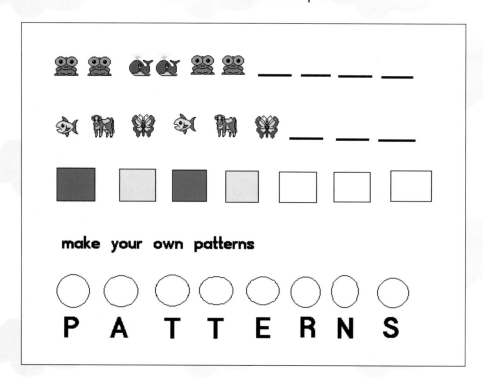

make your own patterns

P A T T E R N S

Line by Line

You can use your straight line tool to make line patterns. Practice drawing these patterns, and then use them to play a game.

Both of these line patterns are called parallel lines. They both go in the same direction and never cross. When they go from side to side, they are called horizontal lines. The train tracks and roads in this computer drawing are horizontal.

When the lines go up and down, they are called vertical lines. The fenceposts and trees are vertical.

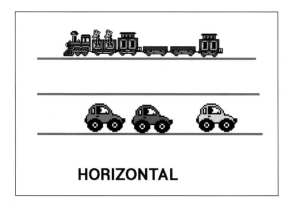

HORIZONTAL

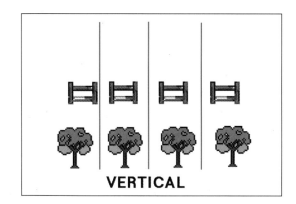

VERTICAL

In your drawing program—

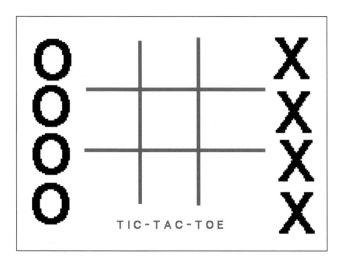

TIC-TAC-TOE

1. Use both kinds of parallel lines to make this pattern. Two horizontal lines go across the page, and the two vertical lines go up and down. Click your straight line tool to draw them.

2. Play Tic-tac-toe with your lines. Use your straight line tool and a fun color to draw your game board.

3. Then click the stamp tool to stamp large Xs and Os to play the game. If you want to take it with you, put 4 Xs and 4 Os next to the board. Print the page. Cut out your markers. You can cover the board with plastic to make it last longer.

4. The first player puts an X in an open square. The other player puts an O in an open square. They take turns until one player has 3 markers in a row.

Your Very Own Coloring Book

You can use your computer tools to make coloring book pages. You can save the picture and color it over and over. If you want, you can make a coloring book page and ask a friend to color it.

In your drawing program—

1. Pick a topic. Our example is a winter snowstorm. Think of some things you might see in a winter snowstorm. Click your thin black pencil tool to draw outlines of these things.

A hill

*Trees
(like Christmas Trees)*

A pond

An ice skater

Two kids on a sled

?

?

2. Now you can color your coloring book page.

3. Use the paint can and spray can tools to color the page on the computer. Make as many coloring book pages as you want. Staple them together to make a coloring book.

Take a look at this!

2 SHAPING YOUR WORLD

Circles, rectangles, squares, and triangles are the basic shapes, but why stop there? Just as you build with blocks, you can build things with computer shapes too. Practice using different drawing tools. Watch how many things you can make without even picking up a pencil (or a pencil tool)!

7

Let's Make Shapes

Start with the shapes that you know.

| Circle | Square | Rectangle | Triangle |

In your drawing program—

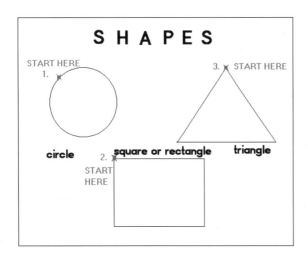

1. Click your circle tool to draw the circle. To start, click your mouse pointer to the top and to the left of the shape, and drag the mouse down and to the right. Make the circle real big.

2. Click the square tool to draw the square or rectangle. Make it about the same size as the circle.

3. Click your straight line tool to draw the three sides of the triangle. Do your shapes look like this?

4. With the letter tool, type the names of the shapes next to them.

5. Use the stamp tool to find pictures with the same shapes. See how many you can find. Stamp one of each picture inside the matching shapes you have drawn.

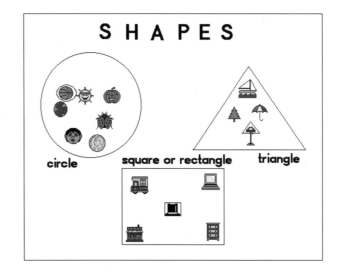

Building with Shapes

Sometimes we see shapes all alone, and sometimes shapes are part of other objects. Many things can be built using basic shapes. Let's try a few.

In your drawing program—

1. Click your square tool and draw two rectangles. Try to draw them the same as the rectangles below.

2. Click your square tool to draw a square on top of the first rectangle and over the second rectangle.

3. The next tool will be the circle tool. Use it to draw wheels. If you make a circle that you don't want, just click your Undo tool or press the Delete key.

4. To finish your picture, color the truck and the wheels. Use the stamp tool to show what this truck might be carrying.

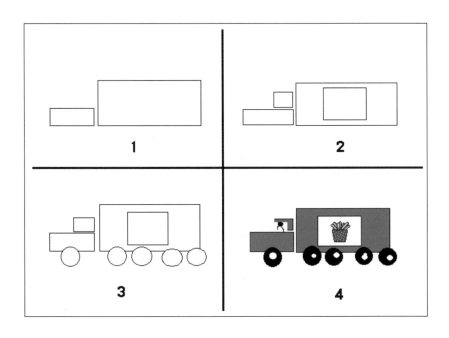

You have made a truck out of shapes.

More Building with Shapes

Let's build something else using shapes. This time make a house using a few new tools.

In your drawing program—

1. Click your square tool to draw a rectangle. Look at the sample here, and try to draw it the same. Click your straight line tool and draw two lines to make a roof on your house.

2. Click your square tool to draw a window and a door. Use your straight line tool to draw panes on the window.

3. The next tool will be your paint can tool. Pick a pattern that looks like a roof, and select black or brown to make that roof pattern. Click your straight line tool and draw a chimney on your roof.

4. To finish your picture, color the house. Use the stamp tool to show people in the doorway. Click your pencil tool to draw smoke coming out of the chimney.

What other things can you draw on your house?
How about a window box, lights?

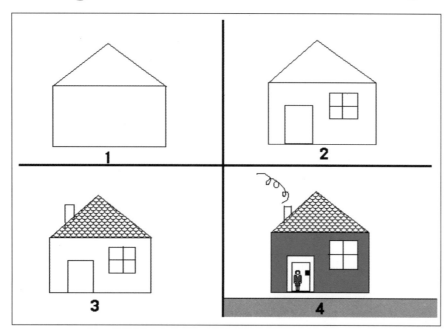

Try other ideas for drawing with shapes—a fire engine, a train, a fruit basket, a sofa and chair, a skyscraper, a race car, a hat, a cat.

Hidden Shapes

We have created some objects (the house and truck) with shapes
of different sizes. This time, let's pick a picture and try to find the
shapes that make it up.

In your drawing program—

1. Choose a favorite stamp. Stamp it on your page and
   make it as large as you can.

2. Find the hidden shapes inside, and draw them next to
   the stamp.

3. Label the shapes and tools. Next time you need a stamp,
   maybe you can make one of your own!

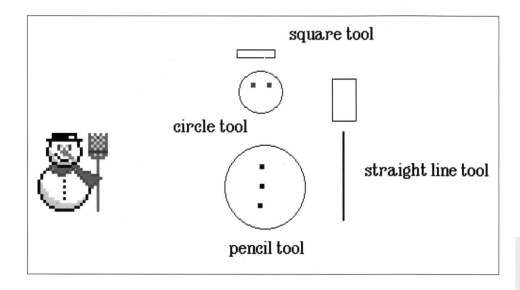

Puzzles Made Easy

What is a puzzle? It is a picture cut into pieces. You can make your own puzzle—just by making a picture on the computer and cutting it into pieces. (For your first puzzle, cut only a few pieces. The next time, you can make more!)

In your drawing program—

1. Draw a fun picture with lots of color for your puzzle.

2. Once you are happy with your picture, click your straight line tool, and make some white lines across the paper to show where the puzzle pieces will be cut. Try to make the pieces all about the same size.

3. When you are finished, take a good look at the puzzle to see how to put it together. Print it.

4. With scissors, cut along the white lines.

5. Try to put the puzzle together.

6. Save all the pieces in an envelope.

GOOD LUCK!

This puzzle has 13 pieces. How about yours?

3 MAKING STUFF
It's a Snap with a Computer!

The computer is our newest tool to make lots of fun stuff. Try each activity once, and then do it all over again in a new way.

Stationery for Kids

Isn't it fun to send notes or letters to your friends and family far away? Now you can design and print your own special set of note cards or stationery. You can then write the notes on the computer or by hand.

In your drawing program—

1. Change your drawing page to a sideways (landscape) position. In most programs, you do this by choosing File, Printer Setup, then Landscape.

2. Use your straight line tool to draw a vertical line (from top to bottom) in the center of the page.

3. You can draw on both sides of the page to make two great note card designs. Add lots of color, stamps, or lines to each note.

4. Print 3 or 4 (or as many as you want) copies of the notes. Cut them along the vertical line and put them all together to make your own set of stationery.

5. If you want to type your notes, save the note card as a file, and click your letter tool to type a note before you print.

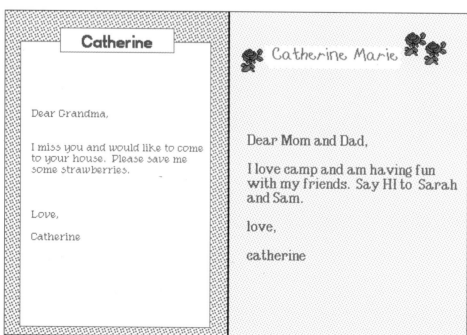

Your Own Cards for Any Occasion

Can't find the perfect birthday, Halloween, or Valentine Day card?
Make your own!

In your drawing program—

1. Change your drawing page to a sideways (landscape) position. In most programs, you do this by choosing File, Printer Setup, then Landscape.

2. Divide your page into 4 equal parts using your straight line tool.

3. In the bottom right corner make the front of your card. Use your letter tool, stamp tool, and any other tool you want.

4. On the top left side, make the inside of your card. Turn the stamps upside down to make this part of the card. Find a tool in your drawing program to do this.

5. Use the paint can tool to fill in colors and patterns.

6. Print and fold your card on the lines. If you want to, go back and CAREFULLY use your eraser tool to erase the lines that divided your page into 4 parts. When you fold your card, you will not see the lines.

Wrapping Paper

For small gifts, you can make your own wrapping paper. Follow along closely!

In your drawing program—

1. Go crazy! Make any design that you want. Use any colors and drawing tools, and keep working until you get what you want.

2. Don't forget—if you want to start over, click File and then New. When you are asked if you want to save, don't save your file. Another way is to erase or "blow up" your whole screen.

3. The idea is to get a great design, and print it as many times as you want. Tape the sheets together, and wrap your present!

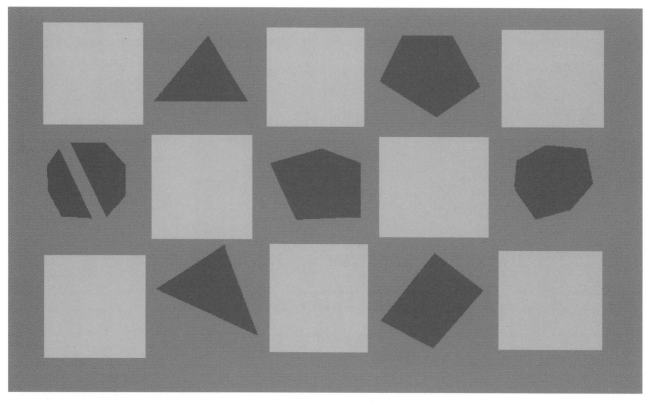

Finger Puppets

Put on a puppet show with your own finger puppets! First, think of a story or theme. Then think of the characters in your story.

To make your own puppets in your drawing program—

1. Hold up one finger against the computer screen and use the pencil tool to draw around your finger. This will make sure that the puppet fits your finger after you print it. (Make sure to draw nice and wide.)

2. Use your color and stamp tools to color in the puppet. Draw a face, hands, feet, hair, and anything else you can think of.

3. You can fit 2 or 3 puppets on one page. When you're finished drawing, print the puppets. Lay the printed sheet on top of a blank sheet of paper and cut around them. Paste the edges of puppet and blank puppet shapes together.

4. Try the puppets on your fingers. If they are too small, erase the outline, draw it wider, and print again.

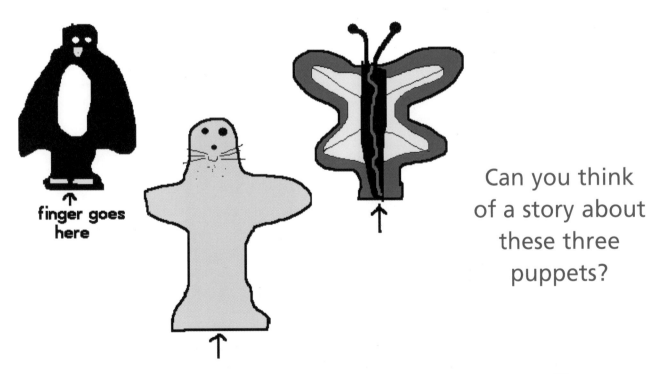

finger goes here

Can you think of a story about these three puppets?

Everybody Needs a Bookmark

Making your own bookmarks can be really fun. You may want to make lots of them to give them as gifts.

In your drawing program—

1. With your square tool, draw a long rectangle in the shape of a bookmark. Use your circle tool to draw a circle near the top to punch out for the string.

2. Draw and color your bookmark using any tools you want. Label it with your name.

3. Print your work.

4. Punch a hole at the small circle and add colorful string. Cover the bookmark with a plastic sleeve and give it as a present to someone special.

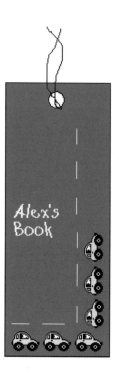

Fancy Frames

A fancy frame will show off those special pictures, projects, or posters.

In your drawing program—

1. Hold your picture or project up to the screen. Click your straight line tool to draw lines around all 4 sides of the picture. If you can, draw the lines a little bit closer to the center of the page. These are the inside lines to your frame.

2. Take the picture away from the screen. Draw the outside lines to your frame. You can draw them as close or as far away as you want from the inside lines.

3. Color and draw between the two lines. Use your letter tool, paint can tool, stamp tool, or any tool you want. You can come up with a theme for your frame that matches what is in your picture.

4. Print the frame. Cut along the outside line, then the inside line. Lay the frame on top of a piece of cardboard, and cut around the outside only. Glue the sides and bottom of the frame to the cardboard. Put your picture in the frame through the top.

The best thing about making your own frames is that you can make them any size or shape. Try some wacky shapes like diamonds, ovals, triangles, or something brand new— and really you!

This is a class from kindergarten.

4 GLAD TO MEET YOU!

Write a storybook about yourself. You can call it "Glad to Meet You" or choose your own title. When you're done, put your storybook in a plastic cover, or staple it together to form a book. The story begins....

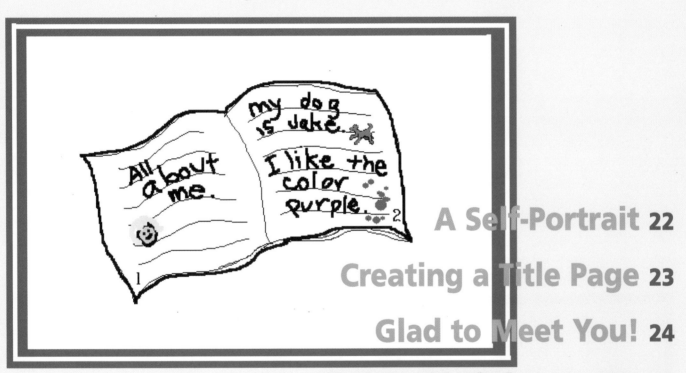

A Self-Portrait

Begin your storybook by creating a self-portrait. Look in the mirror to check the color, shape, and size of your face and its features. Don't forget to notice those extra little things, like freckles, that make you look special.

Make a picture of you in your drawing program—

1. Use the square tool to make a frame large enough to take up most of the page.

2. Click the circle tool to draw your face. Try to make it as real as possible with an oval.

3. Use your circle tool again or the thick pencil tool to form circles for eyes.

4. Click the thick pencil tool to draw outline for lips, and then the paint can tool with red or pink paint for lips.

5. Click the wacky paintbrush tool or thick pencil tool for hair. Choose the right color!

6. Use the wacky paintbrush tool or spray can tool with red for cheeks. With your letter tool write your name on the drawing.

7. Save this picture with your name on the file so you can add this picture into your title page.

Creating a Title Page

What is a title page? It introduces a story and gives us an idea of what the story is about. Create the title page in a word processing program so you can easily center and enlarge your text. If you change your mind, just try it again!

In your word processing program—

1. Make up a title for your story. At the top of the page, type your title.

2. Highlight it and center your title. With the title still highlighted, make the letter size about 32 or 48 point.

MY STORY

Put your
picture
here...

BY
Patty Morgan

3. Choose File and then Import to put your self-portrait from your drawing program into your word processing program. Click and drag the picture to move it around.

4. Put your name at the bottom of the page, and center it.

5. Save and print your work.

Glad to Meet You!

What do you do when you meet someone new? What do you say? You introduce yourself, of course. Practice your introduction and make a picture of you that goes with it.

In your word processing program—

1. Click your letter tool and write some simple sentences. Start by using these fill-in-the-blank sentences:

   My name is _____.

   I am_____years old.

   I like to_____.

2. Save and name your work as a file.

In your drawing program:

3. Create a picture that describes your sentences. In your picture:

   ✎ Draw a background.

   ✎ Draw a building or place.

   ✎ Draw yourself.

   ✎ Draw what you are doing.

   ✎ Add more people and things to make your picture interesting.

4. Save your work as a file.

5. Go back to your word processing program. Open up your file from step 1, and import your picture from your graphics program. Click and drag the picture to place it.

6. Save and print your work.

Happy Birthday to Me

Add a new page to your book about your birthday. Think about the day you were born. Type the day, month, and year.

Here are a couple of ideas that you could write about in your word processing program—

1. You could write about the day you were born.

   ✐ If you can find one, add or draw a picture of a baby. How about a picture of your mom or dad?

   ✐ What else could be in the picture? A hospital? Your crib?

2. You could write about a special birthday that you remember. Maybe you had a great party or went somewhere special.

   ✐ Write your own sentences or use these fill-in-the-blank sentences:

   I was born on _____.

   My birthday is on _____.

   When I was born, _____.

   When I was _____I had a great birthday.

3. Save and print your work.

This is the day I came home from the hospital. My dad said it was the happiest day of his life.

This picture tells about when I was born.

My Birth Certificate

Create your own birth certificate. Pretend it is the certificate that the hospital made when you were born.

In your drawing program—

1. Click the square tool to make a large frame, taking up the whole page.

2. Then use light colors to make a background for your birth certificate.

3. After your background is complete, click the letter tool and choose a letter or font type. Follow this example.

   [Your Name]
   was born on
   [Your Birthday Month, Day, Year]

5. Save and print your work.

Here's a sample birth certificate.

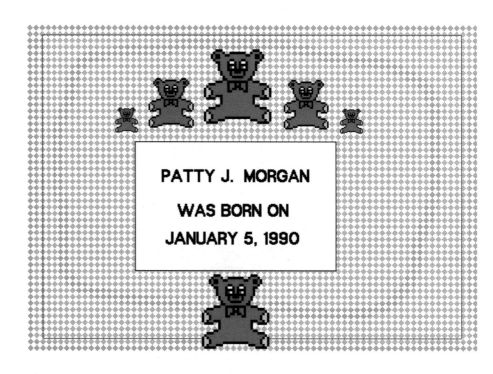

PATTY J. MORGAN

WAS BORN ON

JANUARY 5, 1990

A Neighborhood Map

Draw a map of where you live. You will need to show your street and some of the others near you.

In your drawing program—

1. Click the straight line tool to make the sides of the street. Draw parallel lines. Parallel lines go next to one another in the same direction and never cross.

2. What streets connect to your street? Draw some more straight lines that cross your street.

3. What color should you paint the streets? Try a light gray for asphalt.

4. Is there a traffic light on your street? A stop sign? Check your stamp tools and use them if you can.

5. Put the name on the street, too. For cross streets that go up and down type a single letter, then press Enter (or Return) to go to the next line.
   S (Enter key)
   T (Enter key) and so on . . .

6. Put houses on the street with the house stamps.

7. Paint the house after you stamp it.

8. Click the letter tool to show the house numbers or building names on your street, too.

9. Add scenery (cars, trees, landmarks).

10. Don't forget to save and print your work!

Here's a sample of a neighborhood map.

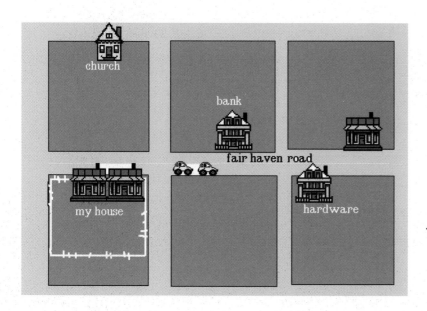

My Family Tree

A family tree shows the family that lives in your house, but also your bigger family—your grandparents, aunts, uncles, and cousins. This is called a family tree, because each part of your family grows like a branch on a tree trunk. Your family tree has two main parts, your dad's family and your mom's family.

In your drawing program—

1. Draw a large tree trunk (fat brown pencil) and 2 main branches (thinner pencil), 1 for your mom's side, and 1 for your dad's side. Leave room at the bottom for roots.

2. Stamp a man and woman next to one another, or draw them. What are your parents' names? Click the letter tool to type their names.

3. Draw roots for the tree.

4. Now, who are your parents' children? Stamp in boys or girls for each root, one for each child in your family. Type in their names with the letter tool.

5. Now let's do your dad's family. Who are your dad's mom and dad? Your grandparents! Stamp a man and a woman near the top of one branch.

6. Did your grandparents have other children besides your dad? These would be your aunts and uncles. Make branches for them and smaller branches above for cousins. Use man or woman stamps and label them with their names.

7. Repeat steps 5 and 6 for your mom's side of the family.

8. When you're finished, click your pencil tool to draw a green tree form around the branches and color it in with the paint can tool.

9. Did you save and print your work?

Look at this sample tree.

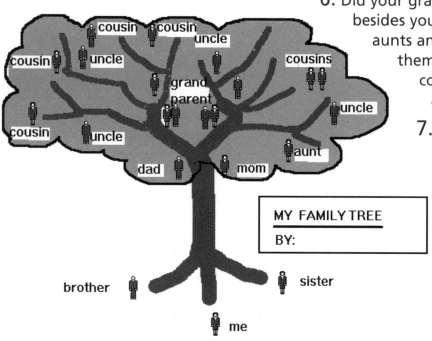

28

5 EXPLORE THE GREAT OUTDOORS

Become a Great Outdoor Explorer by doing these interesting projects that bring the outdoors right on to your computer screen. There's a project for each season of the year. You'll find yourself planning, planting, collecting things, and logging them in. Invite your friends to a scavenger hunt. If you can do it all—you deserve an award!

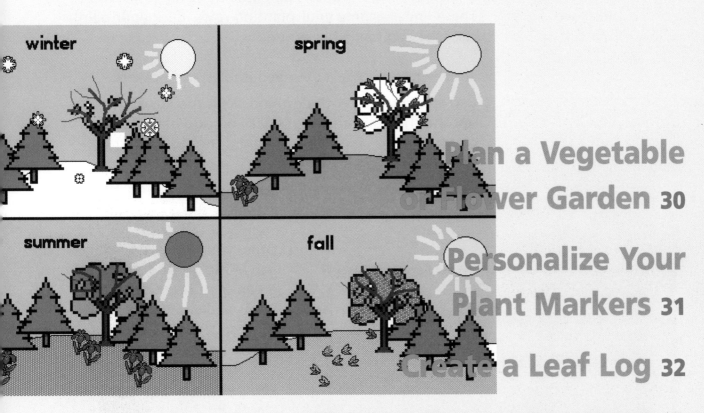

Plan a Vegetable or Flower Garden

What a great idea! First, plan your garden on the computer during the winter. Then buy the seeds and plant in the spring. Start by listing your favorite veggies or flowers. Is your yard sunny enough for tomatoes or tulips? Do you have room for a pumpkin patch?

After your list is complete, draw and label a planting plan for your garden.

In your drawing program—

VEGETABLES
carrots
lettuce

FLOWERS
sunflowers
tulips

1. Click your square tool to draw the outside line of your garden. Make the line thick to be your fence. Use a wide pencil tool to draw some fence posts on your fence.

2. Draw lines from side to side with your thin pencil tool. These lines become your planting rows. Click your paint can tool and paint the ground.

3. Show where to plant your vegetables and flowers.

   Carrots grow under the ground, with the leaves sticking up. Use the paintbrush tool with orange paint for the carrot and a crooked line or stamp tool to draw the greens.

   Lettuce grows above the ground, sometimes in a ball or "head." Use the green pencil tool or the circle tool.

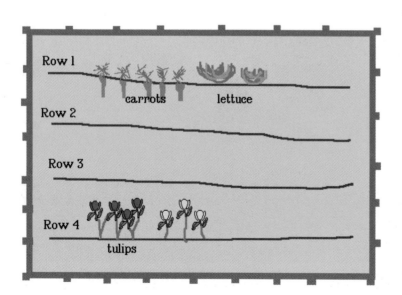

4. Draw your flowers on stems above the ground. Use your green pencil tool for the stems and your paint can or spray tool for the colorful flower petals.

5. Label your rows and garden plants. Print your garden plan and take it with you to buy seeds at the store.

Personalize Your Plant Markers

If you've ever worked with seeds, then you know planting time is in the spring. The seeds are small, you cover them up with dirt, and it usually takes three days to two weeks until they begin to sprout. How will you know where they are? Here's a solution. Make some personalized plant markers to locate and label your planting rows.

In your drawing program—

1. Click your square tool to draw the outside rectangle of the marker. Draw another rectangle just inside that one to make a border.

2. Decorate inside the rectangle by drawing or stamping a picture of the plant you are going to grow.

3. Somewhere on the marker put the name of the plant, and personalize it with your name.

4. Print and cut your marker to the right size. Paste the marker on a popsicle stick. Tie a small plastic bag around the marker so it won't get wet in the garden.

5. Stick the marker in the ground where your seeds are planted. You can plant flower or vegetable seeds in a pot indoors to start. If you do this, stick the marker in the pot, and use the popsicle stick to hold up the plant stems when they start to grow.

peggy's pansies

strawberry patch

Create a Leaf Log

Do you like to collect things and keep track of them? Small details like the date and place you found something, a description of the object, and even a picture of it can be fun to "log in" on your computer. This is how scientists keep track of their discoveries too! Start with a few log pages, and make more as you complete your collection.

These sample log pages are for an autumn leaf collection made when the leaves hit the ground.

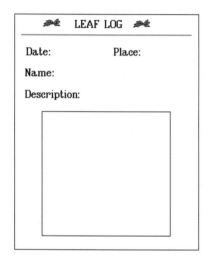

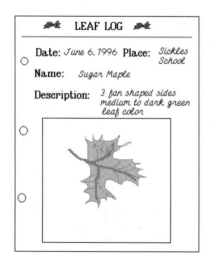

In your drawing or word processing program—

1. Decide what log information is important for your collection. Click your typing tool and write it. Start with these facts and add some more of your own.
   LEAF LOG
   Date:
   Place:
   Name:
   Description:

2. Click the square tool to make a box for your object.

3. You can show the object in your box three different ways.
   • Draw a picture of the object with your pencil tool. Then print your log page.
   • Use a stamp tool or piece of clip art to place a picture in the box. Then print your log page.
   • Print your log page first and glue the actual object in the center of the box.

4. Print as many log pages as you need for your collection. Save this page called **log1**—and print more as your collection grows.

5. Punch holes in the side of your pages. Make a log notebook by tying the pages together with string threaded through the holes.

Go on a Scavenger Hunt

Ever go on a search-and-find mission? Plan your next mission in the Great Outdoors and search through a list of plant parts. Learn to recognize all of these plant parts by drawing diagrams, labeling them, and then going on a scavenger hunt during summer break to search and find samples of them.

In your drawing program—

1. Click your pencil tool to draw a trunk, a stem, branches, and roots.

2. Click your stamp tool to stamp on leaves, buds, and flowers.

3. Click your paintbrush tool to draw needles on the evergreen trees.

4. Click your circle tool to make oval cones.

5. Use your paint can tool to paint the flowers, buds, and grass.

6. Label your plant parts and draw a straight line to point to the correct plant part.

7. Print your diagram and head outdoors to find your samples. Be sure to collect only parts that have already fallen off a plant. Glue each part to the diagram, or if you need more room, use a few pages of the leaf log you made.

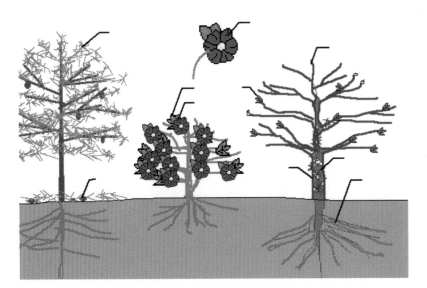

You Deserve an Award!

Congratulations! You have just completed the activities necessary to become a Great Outdoor Explorer. Don't wait for someone else to present the award—do it yourself!

In your drawing program—

1. Click the circle tool to draw the center of the award.

2. Click your pencil tool to draw a design around the circle.

3. Click your straight line tool to draw the ribbons hanging from the bottom.

4. Decorate the award with your drawing tools. Add the name of the award, your name, and any other facts you want.

5. Print the award. Cut it out and pin it to your shirt. Or you can print it on a big label, cut it out, and stick it on your shirt.

6 PLAN YOUR OWN PARTY

You can plan your own party! Pick a theme and then make your own invitations, decorations, and party accessories. Create this with your own home computer. Have fun printing in color or color it yourself. It's party time!

Invitation Station

When you want to have a party, stop by the Invitation Station. What's your theme for the party—is it dinosaurs, dolls, hockey? Be creative. What about party information—pick a date, time, and location. Send out your invitations early! Decide if there's anything that people should wear or bring—bathing suits, baseball gloves, etc.

For a birthday party in October you can use Halloween as your theme. In your drawing program—

1. Draw a picture of a ghost. Save it as a file called **ghost**.

2. After you save the file once as **ghost**, Save As **invitation**. To do this, use the File, Save As command not File, Save. (Save As makes a copy of your file so you don't write over it.)

3. On the **invitation** add whom the party is for, where and when it is, and your phone number—so your guests can call to let you know they're coming.

4. Print as many invitations as you need. You can cut around the shape of the ghost, or fold it into a square.

Let the Decorations Begin

Only your imagination can limit the number of party decorations you can have. Start by thinking of a few...placemats, banners, napkins...and how about cup covers?

PLACEMATS

These will be our placemats for the party.

In your word processing program—

1. Set your page to sideways (landscape) format. To do this, choose File, Printer Setup, then choose Landscape. The placemats will be 8½ inches high by 11 inches wide, the same size as your printer paper.

2. Type "Happy Birthday" and your name. Leave a space for the number of your birthday. Highlight the letters and choose a font type and size. The letters here should be large and colorful.

3. Use the same picture you used on the invitation to make the birthday number. To do this, choose Graphics, or Insert, Picture and look for the name of your picture. (In this case, it's **ghost**.) Import it as many times as you need to get the right number.

4. Print as many placemats as you need for your guests.

5. Buy plastic covers (sheet protectors) to cover them. You can reuse the plastic covers for your next party.

HAPPY
TH
BIRTHDAY
CLAIRE

BANNERS

You need some wall decorations. How about using those ghosts you created for the invitation? Think of different things you can do with the ghost files that you saved.

In your drawing program—

1. Open the **ghost** file, change it to look a little different , and save the new picture with a different file name. You can do this several times to get a variety of ghosts.

2. Print as many copies as you want. Cut them out.

3. To make a banner, string the ghosts together.

A string of ghosts makes a banner across the room.

GOODIE BAGS

Now make the front designs for some goodie bags for your guests.

In your drawing program—

1. Select the **ghost** file and save it with a new name, like **goodie bag.**

2. Decorate **goodie bag** any way you want. You can write "goodie bag" or "Claire's Party" or "Thanks a Lot." You can put your friend's name on the bag too.

3. Print the goodie bag design for as many goodie bags as you need.

4. Cut them out, and glue them to a paper bag. You can tie the tops with ribbon, string, or any colorful way.

The Party's Over

After the party is over, thank everyone for coming to your party and for the gifts. You can have matching thank-you notes ready to send in the mail or deliver yourself. That would be so easy!

In your drawing program—

1. Select or open the **ghost** file that you saved. You can use the ghost as it is, or change the way it looks. If your program has a moving tool you can move it to one side of the page, and write on the other side.

2. Click your letter tool and type your thank-you note.

3. Print out as many notes as you need.

4. Fold each paper in thirds, starting from the top of the page. Hold the paper closed with a fun sticker or piece of tape. Write the name and address on the front, and it's ready to go.

Dear ....,
Thanks for coming
to my party and
for the ....
that you gave me.

See you at school.
Your friend,
Claire

Have a terrific party. Don't forget all of the other parties that you can design yourself . . . pool parties, barbecues, Mother's Day, Father's Day, and many holidays.

7 SPACE ENCOUNTERS

Explore outer space in your own room! With your computer's help, you get to decide what space looks like. You can make many of the parts of the Milky Way galaxy, which is the group of stars and planets we live in. Then you will receive an assignment from NASA and blast off with YOU as the #1 astronaut! (Be sure to save the pictures you draw in this chapter. Later you can decorate a Space Age party, or make up a story about your space adventures.)

Our Solar System

A solar system is made up of all the planets that circle around, or orbit, a sun or star. Earth is just one of nine planets that orbit our sun. The computer is great for drawing planets, because you can draw perfect circles with the circle tool every time. Begin by showing the moon's orbit. Then show the earth orbiting the sun. You can add more planets if you want to: Mercury, Venus, Mars, Jupiter, Saturn, Uranus, Neptune, Pluto. Look them up in your encyclopedia so you can show them orbiting the sun in their right order.

In your drawing program—

1. Click a paint can tool with dark gray paint to paint the whole screen.

2. Use your circle tool to draw the sun (biggest circle), the earth (middle size circle), and the moon (smallest circle).

3. Click your paint can tool to paint the sun yellow, the earth green and blue (to show land and water), and the moon any color you want. Click your circle tool to show the orbits of the moon and the earth.

4. Use your letter tool to label your drawing.

5. Print 2 copies of this page.

6. Cut out the sun, earth, and moon. Paste the two copies of each together, back to back. Punch a small hole in the top of each, and hang them from your ceiling with tape.

Stars That Make Pictures

Astronomers are scientists that study the stars. Many of the earliest astronomers were Greek, and they named many of the stars in groups, after gods and creatures from their myths and stories. The stars are actually not in groups, they just appeared to the Greeks to form patterns in the sky. These patterns are called constellations. Have you heard of Pegasus, Aries, Leo, or Orion the Hunter? Below are pictures of Orion and Pegasus. Can you see why people named the constellations after them? Draw the patterns that these two constellations make in the sky or use a CD-ROM or other encyclopedia to look up and draw other constellations.

In your drawing program—

ORION THE HUNTER

PEGASUS

1. Click a small pencil tool to draw round yellow stars, or draw small stars with the thin straight line tool.

2. Use the thin straight line to connect the stars and show the star pattern.

3. Write the constellation names using the letter tool.

4. Print the page. You can color in the stars with a glow-in-the-dark crayon or marker, and put the paper on the ceiling above your sun, moon, and planets.

Prepare to Blast Off

You've just received a travel assignment from NASA (the National Aeronautics and Space Administration). You will need a special spacecraft to complete your assignment. Here's a diagram of the main parts of a space shuttle. Draw the pieces yourself, print them, and then put them all together. Or, put them together on the computer and then print.

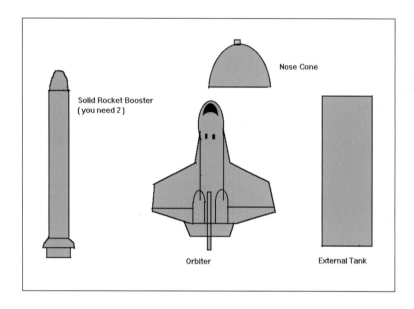

In your drawing program—

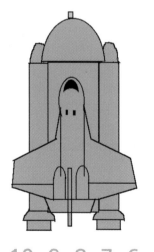

10, 9, 8, 7, 6, 5, 4, 3, 2, 1 Blast off!

1. Click your pencil tool. Draw the shuttle parts just like in the example above.

2. Type a name for your space shuttle on the wing with your letter tool.

3. Label each part, and paint them gray with the paint can tool. Option 1 is to print the parts, cut them cut and paste them together.

4. Option 2 is to use a moving tool to put the pieces together on screen.

5. After you build your shuttle, glue it onto cardboard. Hang it in space from your ceiling, or keep it by your side, ready to blast off at a moment's notice.

Suit Up!

Since NASA wants you to travel on the next shuttle to the moon, you'll need a special suit to protect you in cold outer space, and head gear to provide air to breathe. Draw yourself in space wearing your new protective suit.

In your drawing program—

1. Click your thick gray pencil tool to draw the space suit. Draw the body first, then use a thinner gray pencil to draw the arms and legs.

2. Click the circle tool to draw the space helmet on top of the suit. Use the circle filled with black paint to start, then use a smaller circle with white paint to make the opening.

3. Click the square tool to draw the boots, gloves, life support system, and control panel.

4. Label the parts of the suit and print the page.

5. Find a small picture of yourself, cut out your face, and paste it in the space helmet. Put yourself up in your galaxy, and enjoy your first space walk.

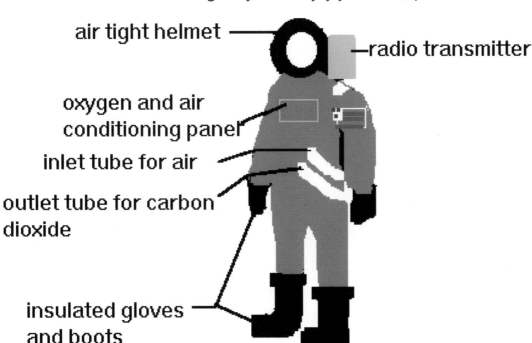

air tight helmet

radio transmitter

oxygen and air conditioning panel

inlet tube for air

outlet tube for carbon dioxide

insulated gloves and boots

An Alien Encounter

Are you alone in space? Look around you and see if you notice any other life forms. Draw what you see.

In your drawing program—

1. Use your drawing tools and your imagination to draw a space alien you might see in space.

2. With the moving tool, click and drag around your alien to select it.

3. Then stamp or copy the picture to make as many aliens on the page as you want.

4. Click your letter tool to write a sentence describing the aliens that you see.

5. Print these aliens, and put them in outer space with you.

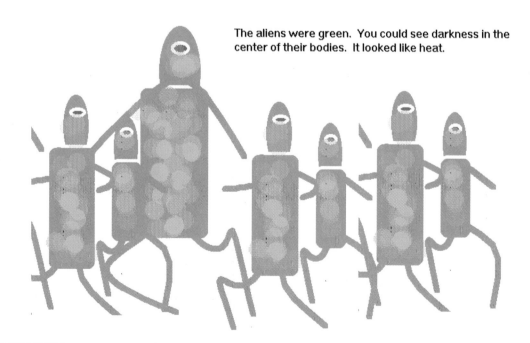

The aliens were green. You could see darkness in the center of their bodies. It looked like heat.

8 SPORTS CLUB

Sports Club is a great way to use the computer. You can work with your friends or alone on your favorite sports or learn about new ones. Go to the sports section of the newspaper, to an encyclopedia, or to an on-line service to get your facts right. Call a few friends and ask them to join the club. Buy some plastic trading card holders and trade your cards. Then go and see a local game together.

Sports Fact Sheets

Chances are you have a favorite sport, and you know a lot about that sport. Why not share your knowledge with your friends?

First, find a picture for the top of your fact sheet. You can use a piece of clip art that came with your program, or you can draw something, save it, and import it in to your sheet by going to a Graphics, Import, Insert, or Image menu. Then look up your sport in the encyclopedia or the sports section in the newspaper and add the most interesting facts to your fact sheet. Answering the questions in this checklist will get you started:

✔ Is it an individual or team sport?

✔ How many players are on each team?

✔ What are the names of the positions?

✔ Where is the sport played?

✔ In what season is it played?

✔ How do you keep score?

✔ Who is a famous person who plays the sport?

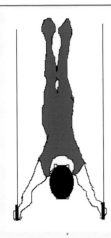

Facts about Gymnastics

Teams	This sport can be both an individual and a team sport. Both men and women compete.
Players	There is no set number of people on a gymnastics team.
Events	There are 6 gymnastics events for men: high bar, parallel bars, pommel horse, vault, floor, and rings. There are 4 events for women: balance beam, uneven bars, vault, and floor exercise.
Scoring	A group of judges give scores from between 0 to 10 (which is a perfect score). Each gymnast must do a required number of moves on each piece of equipment.
Place	Gymnastics competitions are held in gyms.
Famous Players	Nadia Comaneci, Mitch Gaylord, Mary Lou Retton, and Shannon Miller are famous gymnasts.

Sports Equipment

With your friends in the club, talk about all of the equipment used for sports, especially balls! Why is it that so many sports are played with a ball? Draw as many balls for as many sports as you can.

In your drawing program—

1. Draw balls for these sports:

Baseball

Football

Basketball

Soccer

Tennis

Golf

2. Can you draw balls used in other sports? Label your drawing with the name of the sport.

WER'E HAVING A BALL !!!

Draw and label the balls for these sports.
baseball, basketball, football, soccer, tennis, golf,

Trading Sports Cards

Do you like to trade sports cards? You can buy them, or make your own, and buy the plastic card holders to keep them in. Make as many as you want, and trade them with your friends.

In your drawing program—

1. Draw a couple of rectangles on the page that are 2½ inches wide by 3½ inches long, about the same size as a trading card.

2. Print to see if you have the right size for your card holders. Make changes until you get it just right.

3. Find a sports stamp or make a drawing of the sport you are going to work on. On the top of the card, write the person's name with your letter tool. On the bottom, write some sports facts about the person. Use your CD-ROM encyclopedia to look up the facts. When you use the encyclopedia, you can use "word search" and enter in the name of the sport, person, or team you want to write about.

|← 2 1/2" →|

3 1/2"

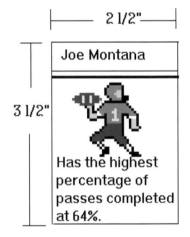

Joe Montana

Has the highest percentage of passes completed at 64%.

Martina Navratilova

In 1984, she won 74 straight matches.

Larry Bird

Led the Boston Celtics in total points and scoring average.

Frank Robinson

Robinson hit 586 career home-runs. He was 4th on the list.

Train for the Olympics!

Olympic Games are an international sports festival that began in ancient Greece. Today, the Olympics take place two years apart. There are summer games, and then, two years later, winter games.

   Summer games—Sports include archery, basketball, boxing, canoeing, kayaking, cycling, fencing, field hockey, gymnastics, swimming, track and field, rowing, shooting, diving, volleyball, weight lifting, wrestling, and water polo.

   Winter games—Sports include downhill and cross-country skiing, biathlon (cross-country skiing and rifle sharpshooting), figure skating, ice hockey, speed skating, bobsledding, and luge. Are any of these your game too? Get ready for the Olympics by making a monthly training schedule for yourself now.

In your drawing program—

1. Click your square tool to make one large rectangle so big that it fills up the page. This is the outside of your monthly calendar.

2. Use your straight line tool to divide this rectangle into 7 columns, one for each day of the week. Do the same thing with rows going across the page, this time dividing the space into 5 rows. (There are never more than 5 weeks in one month.)

3. At the top of each column, click your letter tool and type the days of the week beginning with Sunday.

4. Before you go any further, save your calendar as a file, name it **Olympic1**. You will use this same file to create a new training schedule each month.

5. Continue making your calendar by typing in the month at the top. Now check a real calendar to put the dates on your calendar.

6. Type in your training times. If they are the same for some days, type it once, then highlight it and copy it to another date. This saves you the time of typing the same thing over and over. Decorate the calendar any way you want. You may want to color-code training days.

7. Save this calendar as a file. Name this file the same name as the month it is. The sample is **February 1997.**

8. Print your calendar, and hang it on the refrigerator or in your room. If the schedule changes, just open your file, make the changes, save the file, and print again.

TRAINING SCHEDULE FOR FEBRUARY 1997						
Sunday	Monday	Tuesday	Wednesday	Thursday	Friday	Saturday
						1 2:00-5:00
2	3 3:30-6:00	4	5 3:30-6:00	6	7	8 2:00-5:00
9	10	11 3:30-6:00	12	13 3:30-6:00	14	15 2:00-5:00
16	17 3:30-6:00	18	19 3:30-6:00	20	21 3:30-6:00	22 2:00-5:00
23	24	25 3:30-6:00	26	27 3:30-6:00	28	 2:00-5:00

Write a Sports Article for the Newspaper

How do we find out about what's happening in sports? We hear about sports on radio and television, and read about them in newspapers.

The radio and television usually just report about the major league teams and the scores of the games played the night before. But you can find news about everything from high school games, coaches, and injuries to the latest in equipment in newspapers and magazines.

For your article, you will need:

a catchy headline

a picture

a few sentences about your topic

Here are some ideas for your article:

A sports event that took place last night.

Something that happened at your high school.

An athlete who was named to the Hall of Fame.

Any records that have been set recently in a particular sport.

In your word processing program—

1. Type the headline and "byline" (writer's name).

2. Type your article and change the margins to make it look like it belongs in a newspaper. To do this, highlight the paragraph and change margin settings under File, Page Setup—or Format, Paragraph. Make margins 3 inches on the right and on the left.

3. Highlight your headline, make it bold, and enlarge the font to 48 points.

4. Underline your headline by drawing a horizontal line, or highlight the title and choose Underline from the format menu. Find a piece of clip art in your Graphics menu for your article or click your stamp tool.

Montclair Student to Receive Penn State Scholarship

By [your name]

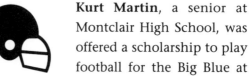

Kurt Martin, a senior at Montclair High School, was offered a scholarship to play football for the Big Blue at Penn State next fall. The offer comes after a banner season for Martin, who plays quarterback for Montclair. He threw 12 touchdowns last season.

9 DINODAYS

Books, posters, videos, cartoons, museum exhibits—all about dinosaurs! It's time to use your computer to show off your creativity and knowledge about these pre-historic creatures. Impress your parents, friends, and teachers with one (or more) of these dynamite dinosaur displays.

Rewrite Dinosaur History

Science books tell us that long ago, there lived a group of animals called dinosaurs. These books show all the facts and figures and pictures of dinosaurs known to date. Wouldn't it be fun to write your own dinosaur book? Don't worry too much about the facts, just have fun telling about dinosaurs your way.

CHAPTER 1: MAN MEETS DINOSAUR

Because dinosaurs lived millions of years ago when there were no human beings, our science books don't show humans with dinosaurs. How big were these animals? Imagine standing next to a dinosaur. Pick a dinosaur you like and draw yourself next to it. Add this page to your dinosaur book.

In your drawing program—

1. Click your pencil tool to draw the outside shape of the dinosaur. Work slowly—it might take a few tries. Click the Undo key if you change your mind.

2. Paint the dinosaur with the paint can tool with any color. Use your paintbrush tool with white and then a black dot on top to make the dinosaur's eye.

3. After the dinosaur is drawn, draw a horizontal line for the ground using your pencil tool. It's always good to draw the ground last so you can make the feet touch the ground.

4. Put yourself in the picture. How much bigger is the dinosaur than you—2 times, 4 times? Add grass, plants, or anything you want to complete your picture.

5. Click your letter tool and write a sentence on your page about the picture.

6. Save this picture as a file called **dino1** and print it.

CHAPTER 2: DISAPPEARING DINOSAURS

Scientists have many different ideas how and why dinosaurs disappeared (became extinct). One idea is that dinosaurs were killed when nearby volcanoes erupted. The ashes blocked out the sun and destroyed their food source. Another idea is that a meteor crashed to the earth and changed the earth's climate, which killed the animals. There are other ideas too. Add a chapter to your book to show how you think the dinosaurs disappeared.

In your drawing program—

1. Click your pencil tool to draw the shape of a volcano. You can use the pencil tool to draw horizontal lines to make the foreground and background of your picture.

2. Click your paint can tool and paint your volcano brown, gray, or black.

3. Use your paintbrush tool, a bubble tool, and the color red to make hot lava spilling out of the top of the volcano. (If you don't have a bubble tool, draw bubbles with a circle tool.)

4. Click the spray can tool with gray paint to make smoke and ash. Show a dark sky covered with ash.

5. Draw some plants near your volcano. When the volcano erupts, the sun cannot shine through the smoke, ash, and dust and the plants die. Be sure your plants look unhealthy!

6. Draw or stamp dinosaurs in your picture near the volcano and the plants. Some dinosaurs need plants for food, and some live by eating other dinosaurs.

7. Write a sentence to explain how these dinosaurs might have been killed. (Hint: What might happen to them when all the plants die?)

8. Save this picture as a file called **dino2** and print it.

CHAPTER 3: A DINOSAUR DISCOVERY

With all of the hundreds of dinosaurs now discovered, surely there can be room for one more. Discover your own dinosaur. Make it fly, swim, or jump—give it big teeth, small teeth, or no teeth at all. Give your new dinosaur a name, then tell the world about it!

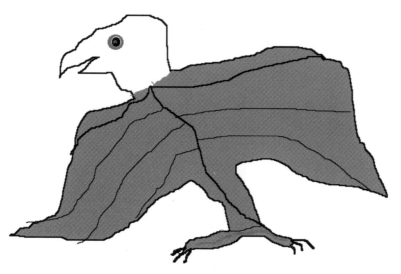

The new dinosaur discoverd high up in the Rocky Mountains is this Swooplodicus. It was named for its keen ability to swoop down and catch fish in the water as they went over the falls.

In your drawing program—

1. Click your pencil tool to draw the dinosaur parts. Draw the head, the teeth, the body, wings, legs, feet, tail, and any other body parts.

2. Click your paint can and paintbrush tools to color the dinosaur.

3. Write a sentence about this new dinosaur discovery of yours.

4. Print your page.

Try each of these chapter projects again and again, using new ideas for each new page of your dinosaur book.

Make a Dinosaur Exhibit

Scientists know about dinosaurs from finding buried fossils, which are traces or impressions of their bones. These fossilized bones are often found when someone is digging up the ground to build a building or road. Some people are actually digging for these fossils. As the fossils are uncovered, scientists can rebuild the forms of the original animals. Many of these fossilized bones are in museums all over the world.

In your drawing program, make a dinosaur exhibit of your own—

1. Click your paint can tool and paint the screen with gray paint. Click your black pencil to draw the outlines of the dinosaur. This outside shape will help you put the bones in the right place.

2. Click your white pencil tool to draw the backbone of the dinosaur. Draw ribs, a skull, and backbones. Each dinosaur will look a little bit different, just have fun trying to make the pieces fit together!

3. When you're finished, label the bones that you know.

4. Create a name plate like the ones you've seen on a museum exhibit for this dinosaur.

5. Print your page.

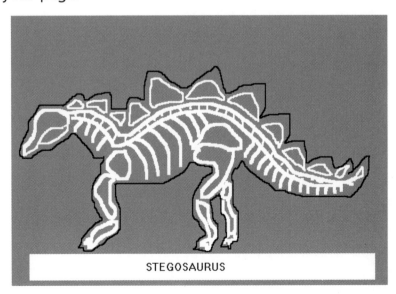

STEGOSAURUS

Welcome to Dinosaur Theater

Read, set, click, and draw a dinosaur movie, video, or slide show on your computer just like a real director. First, decide which dinosaur will be the star of your show. Then create a group of pictures, or scenes, in a row to tell your story. These pictures make up a "storyboard" and they help directors plan their movies. You can use the same scene over and over again to make your storyboard. Just open the last file you worked on, change it, and MAKE SURE TO SAVE IT AS A NEW FILE. To do this, use the Save As command, not the Save command. (Save As makes a copy of your file so you don't write over it.) When you're done, give your story a catchy title, so that everyone will want to see it.

In your drawing program, create a storyboard—

Scene #1

1. Create the scene. Where does your story take place? In the jungle, ocean, city, or in your living room? Use any drawing tools to make this background scene.

2. Label the picture and save the file as **scene1**.

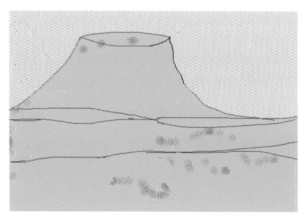

scene 1

scene 2

Scene #2

1. Open the file called **scene1**. Draw the star dinosaur of your show. Show your star sitting, standing, walking, running, sleeping, eating, or whatever.

2. Add some objects to your storyboard that will be used in your show.

3. Label the picture and save the file as **scene2**.

Scene #3

1. Open your storyboard called **scene2,** and change your dinosaur to show some movement. Erase part of your dinosaur with the eraser tool, and redraw it higher or lower.

   Or use a moving tool to move the dinosaur on the page. This is how you show the action of your story.

2. Change or add objects in your picture.

3. Save this picture as a file called **scene3.**

Make as many scenes as you need to finish your storyboard. Print them all. Line them up and tell your story.

The name of this story is *Dinosaur Attacks Desert Homes!*

scene 3

scene 4

scene 5

Dinosaurs once lived in the dry deserts. The Tyrannosaurus Rex was one of the most fearsome. Old movies show dinosaurs attacking cities to protect their young.

10 DESIGN IT YOURSELF!

Welcome to the world of building design, called architecture! You don't mind a little work, do you? Learn how a real building is created and try it yourself on the computer. Prepare to experiment with room sizes, building materials, colors, textures and more.

Set Up Your Office

A person who designs and draws plans for buildings is called an architect. Make believe you are in business to design buildings too. You will need an office. What kinds of things would you need in the office? Think about furniture and tools that an architect might use.

Create a picture of your office. In your drawing program—

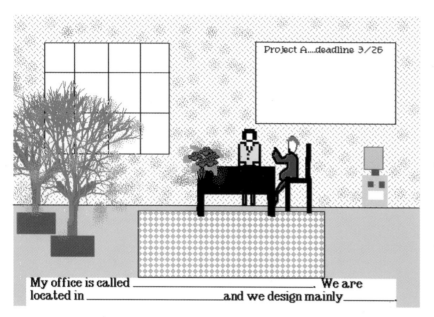

Project A....deadline 3/26

My office is called _____. We are located in _____ and we design mainly _____.

1. Click your straight line tool and draw a horizontal line across the page to show where the floor and wall are connected.

2. Click your paint can tool to paint the walls and floor.

3. Click your square or rectangle tool to draw a desk, a window, and a large bulletin board. Use large stamps to fill up the inside of your office. If you do not have stamps or clip art, draw them yourself.

   Some ideas are a computer, window, bookcase, drafting table, chair, plants, lamps, and people.

4. Click your letter tool and write the name of your office. Write a sentence or two about what you do.

   For office names, use your initials, last name, your town, or a made-up name.

   Examples: PLS Associates, Steinhauser Inc., New York Partners.

5. Fill up your bulletin board with projects you have to do.

Make a Business Card

Almost anybody in business has a business card. Why do you need one? Well, you need one to give to people who might want to use you as their architect. They need to know where to find you and your phone number. The information to be listed on a business card is your name, the name of your company, some kind of graphic symbol or logo (a special creative design which is your company symbol), your address, and your phone number.

Make your own business card in your drawing program—

1. Draw a medium-sized rectangle 2 inches high and 3½ inches wide.

2. Type your name, business name, office address, and your phone number on the card.

3. Add a graphic symbol, logo, or picture. Maybe a house, building tools, or whatever you think goes with your type of business.

4. Save your business card in a file. If your printer can handle it, print on a heavy card stock paper. Cut it out, and you're in business!

5. If you want to make more copies of your card, import the file into a word processing program. Then highlight your graphic box, copy it, then paste it as many times as you can fit on the paper. Then print.

Your First Job

You will design a new home for you and your family. Make a list of the rooms that you need or want in your new house on the computer or with a paper and pencil.

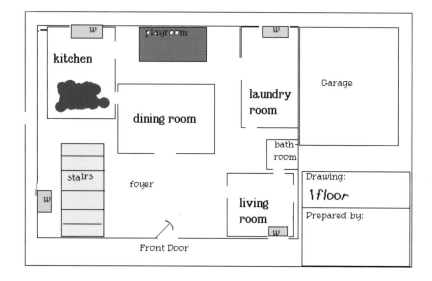

MY NEW HOUSE

ROOMS	NUMBER
Bathrooms	2
Bedroom	4
Kitchen	1
Living Room	1
Dining Room	1
Laundry Room	1
Any Others?	

Now you know what a floor plan is!

In your house, will you have an upstairs and a downstairs? If so, you would have two floors. Decide which rooms will be upstairs and which will be downstairs. In your drawing program, draw the first floor.

1. Click your square tool to draw a large rectangle. (It should take up the whole page.)

2. Click your straight line tool to make walls in your house. Think about which rooms are small and which are big. (For example, bathrooms are usually smaller than living rooms, kitchens, and family rooms). Leave an opening in the walls for the doors.

3. When you have all the rooms you want, click your letter tool and label them. You can also stamp in some things that you might use in that room.

4. Decide where you want to have windows in your house. Go to all 4 sides and put a "W" where you want to have a window.

5. Label your plan "First Floor Plan" and "Prepared By [your name]," or "[your last name] Residence."

What's an Elevation?

An elevation shows what you see when you are facing a building. A front elevation shows the front of a building from the street. You cannot see the sides or back of the building. If you are drawing an elevation of your building, you will draw only certain things like windows, shutters, roof, door, and chimney. (Look outside at your neighbor's house. What things do you see?)

In your drawing program, draw an elevation—

1. Draw a large rectangle with the square tool. This is the outline of your house.

2. Using your straight line tool, draw connecting lines on top of your outline for the roof. Paint the roof.

3. Click your square tool again to draw the windows and doors in your house. (They should be in the same place you wanted them in your floor plan.) An elevation would show both the first and second floors. Hint: architects usually make the windows line up. Then draw a chimney if you want one.

4. Will you have shutters on your windows? If so, draw and paint them with the paint can tool.

5. Paint your house now. Think about textures for the roof and for the side of your house. Is it wood? Is it brick? If you have tools to show these things, click them with the colors you want.

6. Click your stamps or drawing tools to put in a sidewalk or trees in front of your house. (Not too many though, we want to see your building!)

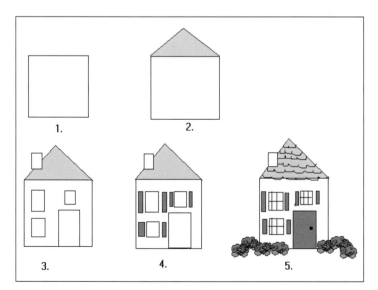

Make a Building Out of Shapes

To draw things, including houses, you can combine several shapes to make what you want. Start with basic shapes—triangle, square, rectangle, and oval. Draw these shapes on a page and move them around to make things that look like a building.

In your drawing program—

1. Make a couple of each of the shapes you know.

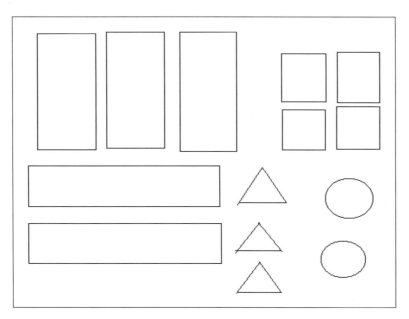

2. Use your moving tool or moving commands to move the shapes around the page until they form a building.

3. Connect the shapes with lines.

Does this group of shapes look like a building to you?

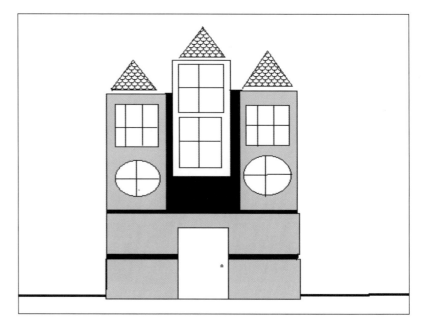

Other Types of Buildings

Architects create other types of buildings besides houses. Think of some other types. Churches, shopping centers, movie theaters, banks, office buildings, schools. As your town's architect, you have been asked to create and draw a shopping center with three stores.

In your drawing program—

1. Draw a large rectangle for the building outline. Use your straight line tool to divide the building into 3 sections, one for each store.

2. Click your square tool to add 3 doors, one to each section.

3. Make the roof lines. How many peaks will you have? Fill the roof with a textured paint.

4. How many windows will you have? Decide how much light you will have in the building. Click your square tool to add windows. Use your straight line tool if you want to add window panes.

5. What is the name of your shopping center and what will the stores sell? Click your letter tool to put these names on your building.

6. Paint your building with the paint can tool, and stamp on any details to help show customers what you sell.

11 ANCIENT EGYPT

Ancient Egypt brings to mind pictures of pyramids, stone carvings, tombs lined with treasures, and other signs of a civilization long ago. Try recreating the world of ancient Egypt from the many clues the Egyptians left behind. Print the drawing from each of the following clues, and put them all together. Cut them out, then build a diorama, or attach your creations to a poster-board or wall to make your own ancient Egyptian civilization or museum exhibit. You can build an Egyptian vocabulary, too!

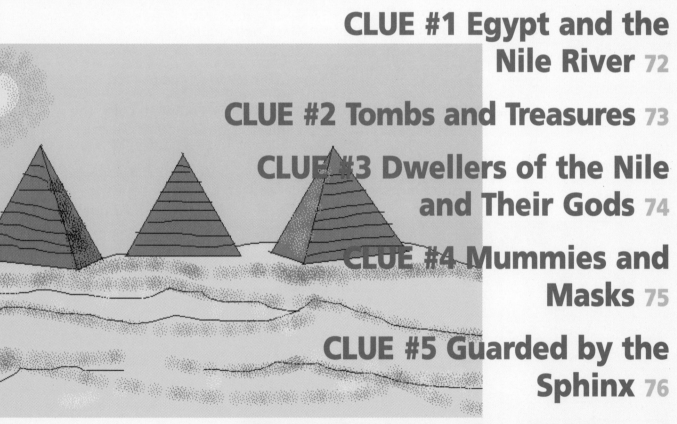

CLUE #1 Egypt and the Nile River

The Nile River flows through the center of the country of Egypt on the African continent. The Nile River begins in the country of Uganda and flows to the north and empties into the Mediterranean Sea.

   The Nile River valley is fertile land and good for agriculture. The fertile river valley is surrounded mainly by desert. Can you see why the people of ancient Egypt built their communities here?

fertile—
   able to produce crops and plants plentifully and easily

desert—
   a barren region with little or no rainfall

Draw the Nile River valley with your drawing program—

1. With a computer or hardcover encyclopedia, look up Egypt, Africa, or Middle East. Find a map of this area.

2. Click your thin black pencil tool to draw the outlines of the Middle Eastern countries.

3. Use your thick blue pencil tool to draw the Nile River. Outline it with a thin black pencil line.

4. Color the land brown.

5. Click your spray can tool with green paint to color the fertile banks of the Nile River.

6. Label these water bodies—Mediterranean Sea, Persian Gulf, Red Sea, and the Nile River. Label the countries—Egypt, Saudi Arabia, Sudan, Ethiopia, and Uganda.

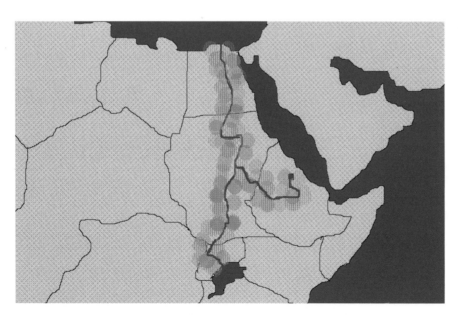

CLUE #2 Tombs and Treasures

The Egyptian left us a landscape of huge stone pyramids. The pyramid was used as a tomb for the burial of pharaohs. This is your second clue.

   In addition to the pyramid above ground that you see, a chamber beneath the earth contains the body of the pharaoh. Along with the body was buried some of the treasures that the soul would need to take to the "afterlife" or place after death. These possessions included food, clothes, furniture, paintings, and jewels.

tomb—
   a grave or place of burial

pyramid—
   a solid shape with a square base and triangular sides which meet at a point

Draw Egyptian pyramids in your drawing program—

1. Click your straight line tool to draw the sides of the pyramids.

2. Show two of the pyramids in 3 dimensions, so that you can see 2 sides.

3. Color the pyramids brown, the sand beige, and the sky blue.

4. Leave 1 of the pyramids open. Draw or stamp some of the treasures you might want to take with you to the afterlife.

CLUE #3 Dwellers of the Nile and Their Gods

Inside these ancient pyramids are wall paintings and carvings showing what the Egyptian people did. Your third clue is the many wall paintings left by the Egyptians.

The dwellers of the Nile River Valley worshiped many gods. Their gods were sometimes represented by creatures that appeared in their daily lives like birds or animals and were sometimes like humans. Some gods were a combination of both. Gods were rain-makers, justice makers, or gods of the sun, the earth, the sky, war, and the underworld.

dweller—
a person who resides or lives somewhere

gods—
beings thought of as superior in nature, considered worthy of worship

In your drawing program create a wall painting to show people worshiping an ancient god—

1. Draw the outline of the heads and bodies using the thin black pencil tool.

2. Use a thicker black pencil tool to draw the dark lines along the eyes. Pictures of Egyptian gods and goddesses often show them with sharp eye lines.

3. Draw colorful lines around the collar of the clothing of the worshiper and the god.

4. Fill in the dark hair and clothing with the paint can tool.

5. Decorate the walls yourself with some ancient symbols.

CLUE #4 Mummies and Masks

When Egyptian pharaohs (kings) died, their bodies were prepared in a special way for burial. The bodies were "mummified"—they were dried out and wrapped in linen bandages to preserve them. A mummified body was then placed in a series of caskets and then in a tomb. This is your fourth clue.

One famous pharaoh was King Tutankhamen (King Tut for short). King Tut lived from 1370 to 1352 B.C.E.—he died when he was only 19 years old. He was mummified, and his head was then covered with a decorative funeral mask.

mummy—
   a dead body preserved from decay

dynasty—
   a series of rulers, a line of kings or princes

Have some fun wrapping your own mummy and recreating a gold funeral mask in your drawing program—

1. Draw the outline of a body with a thin black pencil tool.

2. Click a thick pencil tool with the color gray or beige to represent pieces of cloth and wrap the body. Draw as many of the cloth pieces as you want to create your mummy. Print and cut out the mummy.

3. Click your black pencil tool again to draw the outside of the mask.

4. Use a thicker line pencil to draw horizontal stripes around the headpiece. Draw thick lines around the eyes.

5. Paint the mask gold with your paint can tool, and decorate the mask any way you want. When you're finished, print the mask and cut it out. Put the mask over the mummy's face.

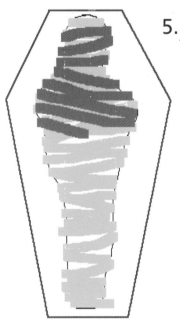

CLUE #5 Guarded by the Sphinx

Guarding the entrance to many Egyptian tombs and temples are statues carved out of stone. Some are in the form of a sphinx, a lion's body with a human head. The head of the sphinx looked like the head of the pharoah whose temple or tomb the sphinx guarded. Some historians say that the sphinx symbolizes the force and wisdom of the pharoah. This is your fifth and last clue.

temple—

a building used for the service or worship of a god or gods

Carve your own sphinx in your drawing program—

1. Click your pencil tool to draw the outline of the sphinx. Notice the angle of the lion's paws—this angle helps to show the object in 3 dimensions.

2. Draw some lines for eyes, nose, and mouth with the pencil tool.

3. Draw horizontal lines to show the body of the statue. Add the lion's paws.

4. Use your paint can tool to color the statue with a sandy color. Then use the spray can tool to darken or lighten places where the statue is in shadow or sunlight.

5. Complete the picture by drawing the entrance to the temple behind the sphinx. Add a background that shows what a desert area would look like (sand, hot sun, wind).

6. Print your sphinx.

Hieroglyphics—the Writing of Ancient Egyptians

Hieroglyphics are pictures the Ancient Egyptians used to write with. They used hieroglyphics for over 3,500 years, until they began to use the Greek alphabet. Hieroglyphic writing represents letters and sounds.

Here are the letters of the alphabet in hieroglyphics. Use them to practice writing some words. You can also use this system to write notes to your friends. Just make sure they have a copy of this chart in order to translate your notes!

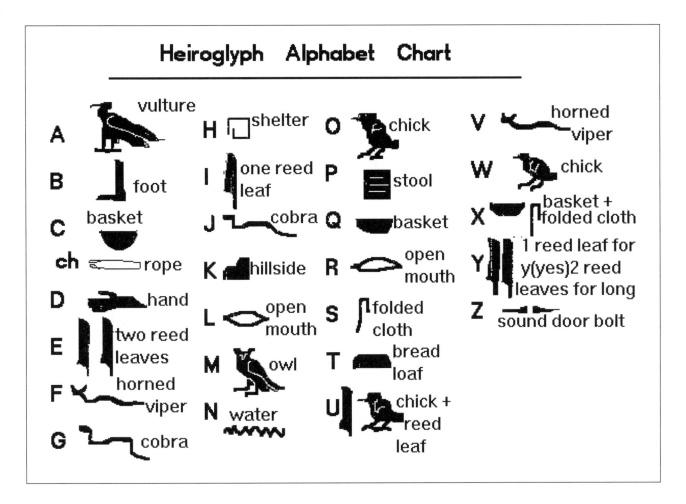

Heiroglyph Alphabet Chart

- A — vulture
- B — foot
- C — basket
- ch — rope
- D — hand
- E — two reed leaves
- F — horned viper
- G — cobra
- H — shelter
- I — one reed leaf
- J — cobra
- K — hillside
- L — open mouth
- M — owl
- N — water
- O — chick
- P — stool
- Q — basket
- R — open mouth
- S — folded cloth
- T — bread loaf
- U — chick + reed leaf
- V — horned viper
- W — chick
- X — basket + folded cloth
- Y — 1 reed leaf for y(yes) 2 reed leaves for long
- Z — sound door bolt

In your drawing program, write these words by drawing the symbols above with your black pencil tool.

SECRET CODE

MEETING TOMORROW

12 TROPICAL RAINFORESTS

The rainforests have long been a place of study for scientists, authors, nature lovers, and many others. Why are they interested in rainforests? One reason is that they are the source for so many foods, medicines, and materials that can be used by people. Another reason is that rainforests contain many of the trees on the planet, which help keep the air we breathe clean. So we say, "Save the Rainforest," and hope that it will remain as it is for all of us to use, explore, and learn about for years to come. Come on a journey inside a tropical rainforest, and create some of the natural wonders you might find there yourself.

Where Are the Tropical Rainforests?

Tropical rainforest areas are located around the equator, an imaginary line that passes around the earth at an equal distance from the north and south poles, where the climate is often warm and wet. Rainforest areas typically receive more than 100 inches of rainfall in one year. By comparison, the United States usually receives no more than 60 inches of rainfall in any one place. Many times, rainforest areas are located in or near a river basin, where the soil is moist and plant life is plentiful.

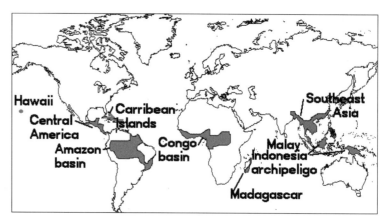

The Amazon rainforest is the world's largest tropical rainforest. It surrounds the Amazon River basin in South America. Look up Amazon River or South America in your encyclopedia.

In your drawing program—

1. Create a map of your own based on this example or on what you find in the encyclopedia.

2. On your map, fill in the names of the countries in South America that are near the Amazon River. Name the oceans on your map too.

Now let's go inside the rainforest!

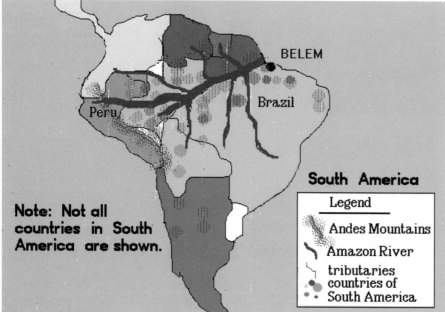

Note: Not all countries in South America are shown.

Under the Canopy

The rainforest is a dense world with various layers of plants. The layers of the rainforest can be broken down into smaller layers—the upper layer or canopy, the understory, and the rainforest floor. These layers have different levels of light, moisture, and animal and plant activity. There are two ways to create your own rainforest with the next four activities. One, print on regular paper and make a collage. Two, show the different layers of the rainforest by printing on a type of clear paper called a "transparency." First check that your printer can handle transparencies. You can buy them at a copy shop or stationery store. Then use this outline as a guide for drawing each layer. After you print, lay the transparencies on top of each other to create a tropical rainforest you can actually see through. Be sure to print each layer separately.

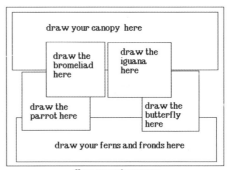

Your computer screen

Let's look at the rainforest more closely. The canopy is made of the branches and leaves of tall trees. They form an umbrella-like covering which creates a home for many birds and animals. The rainforest canopy does not allow much sunlight to filter through to the forest floor.

To draw your own canopy in your drawing program—

1. Click your wide brown pencil tool to draw the trunks of 2 or 3 trees. Then click a narrower pencil to add some branches. Try using 3 or 4 pencils, getting smaller as you get to the end of the branches. Remember to draw this rainforest layer at the top of your page.

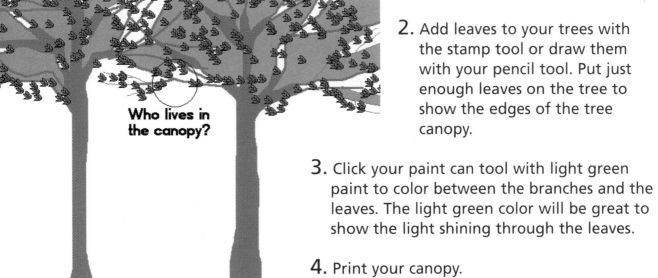

Who lives in the canopy?

2. Add leaves to your trees with the stamp tool or draw them with your pencil tool. Put just enough leaves on the tree to show the edges of the tree canopy.

3. Click your paint can tool with light green paint to color between the branches and the leaves. The light green color will be great to show the light shining through the leaves.

4. Print your canopy.

Animals of the Rainforest

Pretend you are looking through an imaginary pair of binoculars, and discover what might be living high up in the rainforest canopy.

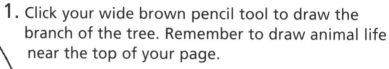

To draw this lizard (called an iguana) in your drawing program—

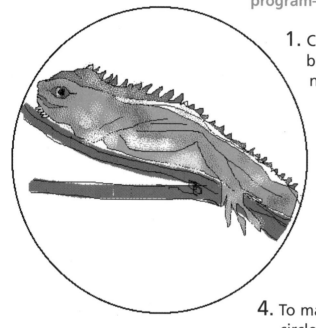

1. Click your wide brown pencil tool to draw the branch of the tree. Remember to draw animal life near the top of your page.

2. Click your thin black pencil tool to draw the outside of the iguana and the inside lines, the eye, and the lines in the branch. Color your iguana with your paint can tool.

3. Click the spray can tool with yellow, brown, and dark green to show color change, shade, and shadow in the iguana. The color white in the spray can tool will tone down the color green in the skin of this animal.

4. To make the eye, draw the outside of the eye with the circle tool. Leave a light color (white or yellow) outside and black for the pupil of the eye.

5. Write a sentence about the iguana, a canopy dweller.

To draw this brightly colored bird in your drawing program—

1. Use your black pencil for the parrot outline.

2. Click your paint can tool to paint the yellow and blue areas of the body and the brown of the branch.

3. Click the circle tool with no color in the fill area to draw a circle around it.

4. Use the spray can tool to blend the colors of blue, yellow, and gray. Use the gray to create shadows on the bird.

Bromeliads and Butterflies

Beneath the canopy of the trees is another level of plant and animal life called the understory. Plants and animals that live here do not need the sunlight of the canopy, but they would not survive in the darkness of the forest floor. Some of the most brilliant and beautiful inhabitants of the rainforest live just "in between." Bromeliads (broh-mee'-lee-ads) are some of these amazing plants. They have both flowers and leaves, and they grow on tree trunks or on other plants in the understory.

In your drawing program—

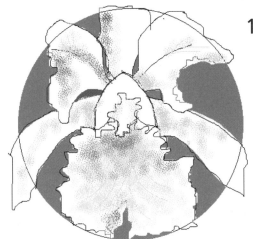

1. Click your thin pencil tool to draw the black outside lines of this bromeliad. Remember to draw it in the center of your page.

2. Use your spray can tool to shade, shadow, and texture the plant. Notice that near the center and the intersection of plant leaves, the colors are shaded more deeply.

3. Color the background a dark color, so that you can see the inside of the flowers better.

Butterflies in the rainforest of South America are among the world's largest.

In your drawing program—

1. Use your pencil tool and your imagination to draw this beautiful butterfly. The colors can be many and the design unique to you.

2. To draw the leaf, outline with the black pencil tool and fill in with color from the paint can tool. Use a light green thin pencil tool to draw the fine lines along the leaf.

Ferns and Fronds

The rainforest floor is a rich combination of decaying plants and a tangled web of roots from living plants which feed on the decaying ones. Ferns thrive in the moist dark environment of the rainforest floor. Their leaves are called fronds, and they have spores on the underside of the leaves to create new ferns.

In your drawing program—

1. Click your thin black pencil tool to draw the center lines of the ferns near the bottom of the page. Then use the same pencil tool to draw the fronds. The top of the leaves should be narrow and get wider near the roots.

2. With your black pencil tool, draw the line of the ground. Click your paint can tool to color it in a deep rich brown.

3. Use your paint can tool with dark green to color underneath and at the bottoms of the ferns. These areas of the plant get the least amount of light.

4. Click the paint can tool with light green to color the top of the leaves. These areas get the most light.

5. Click your spray can tool with a dark color and then light to spray around and mix the colors. This will show the sun reflecting off the plants. Spray some light green color into the air to show the reflection of other plants.

People of the Rainforest

Some native people of the rainforest still live the way their ancestors did, while others live in towns and cities. Use your encyclopedia to learn more about the lives of native people of the rainforest, and then use your imagination to write a letter to an imaginary rainforest penpal. Make sure you are in a word processing program, and follow this outline or create one of your own.

Then, if you really like to write letters and get mail, write to the address below and ask for a list of penpal organizations. Soon you'll be able to write to your new friends in the Amazon (or Japan, or South Africa, or . . .)!

US Committee for UNICEF
Education Department
333 East 38th St.
New York, NY 10016

[Date]
(Enter)
(Enter)
Dear _____:
(Enter)
(Enter)
I am writing to you because you live in a wonderful place. I would like to come there someday. _____

_____.

(Enter)
In my country, there are many cars, buses, and houses. There are stores to shop in and we have many helping services like schools, police stations, fire stations, and hospitals. _____

_____

(Enter)
(Enter)
Best wishes to you and your family,
(Enter)
(Enter)
Sincerely,
[your name]

Take Rainforest Action

Create a poster of your own with a picture and a couple of sentences about the rainforest.

In your word processing program—

1. Type your title in all capitals, (use Caps Lock), highlight the text, and center it.

2. Create a picture in your graphics program and save it with a file name. Place your mouse pointer below your title, and add the picture by clicking Graphic, Image, or Insert Picture.

3. Type the rest of your poster message, highlight the text, and center it.

WHAT'S SO SPECIAL ABOUT THESE TREES?

These trees protect the plants of the tropical rainforest. The plants provide food for the rainforest animals. So, please save these trees.

13 PC PUBLISHER

The possibilities of using your computer to draw and write are endless. This is your chance to combine the two and be a desktop publisher. Think of all the things you could publish—newspapers, magazines, advertisements, newsletters—the list goes on. Publish a newspaper of your own!

Newspaper Publisher

Newspapers contain news that is happening around the world. There are so many different kinds of news stories . . . international, national, local, human interest, humorous, and other stories. Besides stories, there are some other sections in the newspaper.

Business—stock market, commodities market, business information

Classified—advertisements for employment (help wanted), sales of cars and merchandise

Comics—comic strips or panels

Lotteries—announcements of lottery numbers and winners

Movies—movie theater schedules, listings, and advertisements

Puzzles—crossword and word-find puzzles

Television—local and national TV station schedules and show news

Let's start on the front page. This could be the most important part of the paper, because it gets people's attention and encourages them to buy and read the paper. Let's look at the outline of a front page.

- Name of the paper
- Date and price
- Headline
- Feature story
- By whom?
- View into what's inside

Learn how to create your own front page in your word processing program—

1. Type your paper's name, highlight or select, center, change font size to large (36–42 pt.).

2. Type the date, tab to the center, type the date the paper began, tab to end of line, type the price. Highlight and change font (10–12 pt.).

3. Type your headline (32 pt.), highlight and center, change to medium font (26 pt.).

4. Define your columns for the newspaper by clicking on Format, Columns or Format, Section, Columns. Then choose 4 (or any number of columns you want).

5. Type article title, highlight and select medium font (18 pt.) and bold.

6. Type your byline and job title. Highlight your name and make it small font (8 pt.).

7. Type your article (10 pt.), highlight the text and click on Format, Full Justification. This should make your text line up on both the left and the right.

8. Import a graphic image.

9. Type your title, highlight and center. Insert a bullet or character, and type your information. Press Enter twice to get below the paragraph. Select the paragraph and format with a border.

10. Import a graphic image, and put a border around it. Type a caption for the image.

THE NEW AGE NEWS

January 12, 1997   Since 1904   Price 75 cents

East Coast Buried in Snow!
Residents of 10 States Still Digging Out

Turnpike Closed for the First Time in 20 Years

By Tom Starr
STAFF WRITER

There wasn't much traffic moving yesterday on the state turnpike. Officials warned drivers to stay off the roads, and that's exactly what they did. That warning, and a threatened $50 fine for non-emergency vehicles found on the road, worked as a deterrent to keep people home so road crews could clean off the roads. It took nearly 24 hours, and the roads are finally becoming clear enough for some employees to get back to work.

MORE STORM COVERAGE INSIDE

- *How much snow did we get?*
- *Are we expecting more?*
- *State totals*

TODAY'S GARDENING TIPS
Please see GARDENING, page 13.

Try a Sports Page

Sports sections of the newspaper include articles, statistics, schedules, and information about different sports. Timing is important, so that information about yesterday's game is in today's paper. . . . You get the idea.

Create a headline for the sports page just like you did for the front page. Then create one of each of these: an article, a schedule, and a chart with statistics. You're on your own as far as type sizes and styles. Have fun!

In your word processing program—

1. Type your article title. On the lines below, add your byline and the city you are writing about.

2. Type or import your article (remember to select Full Justification).

3. Type the chart title and any headings you need on the line below the title.

4. Type the teams, underline 4 or 5 spaces, type the statistic number, hit spacebar 4 times, type number, etc. Finish the statistics yourself.

5. Import a graphic. Create a caption.

6. Type a schedule title. On the next line, draw a horizontal line.

7. Type game information, tab, type the game time. Complete this schedule on your own.

SPORTS

NETS AND SONICS ON A ROLL IN NBA

By Jerry Jackson

NEW YORK—The New Jersey Nets and the Seattle Supersonics have the best records in the NBA. In the Eastern Conference, the New Jersey Nets have sole possession of the conference's best record, and they're in first place, too! Same thing with the Supersonics—they, like the Nets, are 81–1, their one loss coming to the Nets. (The Nets' one loss came to the Sonics.) The Sonics are coming off two early play-off exits, and the Nets have been unable to make the play-offs lately in the NBA. Looks like a championship will be coming soon.

Today's cycling news inside!

AMERICAN LEAGUE

East	W	L	Pct.	GB
New York	37	26	.587	—
Baltimore	35	28	.556	2
Boston				
Toronto				
Detroit				

Central

Cleveland

Chicago

Milwaukee

Minnesota

Kansas City

West

Texas

Seattle

California

Oakland

NATIONAL LEAGUE

Schedule of Today's Games

Los Angeles at Atlanta
1:05 pm
San Diego at Chicago
4:05 pm.

Now for the Comics

Believe it or not, this is a favorite spot for many readers.

To make your comic strip in your drawing program—

1. Brainstorm for ideas for a comic with 3 or 4 frames. Each frame should have at least one person, place, or thing that is the same as the previous frame to help your reader follow the action.

2. Create the first frame of your comic strip. Use any drawing tools that you need. Draw a conversation bubble to put words in the characters' mouths.

3. Save the drawing with the filename **comic1**.

4. Open the file called **comic1** and save as **comic2**. Now you can change anything you want or add to the new picture. Save the file again when you are finished. This will be frame 2 of your comic strip.

5. Open the file called **comic2** and save as **comic3**. Change anything you want or add to the picture. Save the file again when you are finished. This will be frame 3 of your comic strip.

6. Now you're ready to add the comics to the rest of your newspaper. In your word processing program, import the 3 graphic files, one by one. Line them up in a row, and there's your comic strip. Put a box or border around each frame.

Advertising for Anything

Advertising makes people aware of a product's good qualities. Advertisers sometimes use a slogan or catchy phrase to get your attention. Think of some advertisements or commercials that you remember. Plan your own advertisement with these things in mind.

In your word processing program—

This can be your advertising outline:

- special price or savings
- name of the product
- slogan
- facts about the product

1. Use your graphics function to draw a picture of the product. Or import a picture you made in your drawing program.

2. Type a slogan for the product to get attention.

3. Add some facts about the product, especially things that are great.

4. Type any special prices or savings, coupons, or promotions: Buy one, get one free! 20% MORE! New Bigger Box!

5. Include locations of places where the product can be purchased.

NEW!!!

20% More!

Good Morning Cereal

MAKE YOUR MORNING MORE THAN GOOD!!!

Fresh crispy flakes of corn with natural raisins and nuts mixed right in. Low in fat and calories, great for the kids.

the new cereal.....
crispy flakes with nuts & raisins

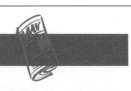

SKILL BUILDER INDEX

Activity Title	Age	What They Create	Development Skills	Computer Tools/Skills
1. Play Games with Colors and Patterns	5–6	make games to play on computer, Tic-tac-toe, shapes, color matching	tools, parallel, horizontal, vertical, colors, primary, secondary, top, bottom, left, right.	spray can, straight line, typewriter, paint can, pencil, square, stamp, circle
2. Shaping Your World	5–6	shapes, circle, rectangle, triangle, oval, puzzles	tools, labels, matching early graphs, sequence and order	circle, square, straight line, stamps, paint can
3. Making Stuff: It's a Snap with a Computer!	5–6	make bookmark, puppet, wrapping paper, frames, stationery, note cards	inside, outside, left, right, estimating center	paintbrush, undo, typewriter, pencil, square, circle, printing to card stock paper, landscape printing
4. Glad to Meet You!	5–8	a story—title page, introduction, birth certificate, family tree, fill-in-the-blank sentences	concept of self, introduction to maps, horizontal, vertical, east, west, parallel	outline, fill in, background, foreground
5. Explore the Great Outdoors	5–8	garden plan, awards, scavenger hunt, diagrams, logs	labeling, seasonal concepts, using encyclopedia, plant parts	spray can, multiple printing, saving files, printing to label paper
6. Plan Your Own Party	5–8	make invitations, placemats, thank-you notes, decorations	organization skills, process	typewriter, saving and retrieving files, moving tool, multiple printing
7. Space Encounters	6–8	solar system, constellations, shuttle diagram/design	concepts of distance and size, working with other materials	spray can, multiple printing, moving tool, copying, saving files
8. Sports Club	6–8	club, members—sports, newspaper article, trading cards, calendar	using encyclopedia, scheduling, making a checklist, creative writing	square, stamp, edit stamp, typewriter, margins, importing graphics, copy and paste, underline
9. Dinodays	6–8	create movies, slide show, museum exhibits, history book	reptile family, skeleton, herbivore, carnivore, sequence and order, simple sentences	shade, texture, depth, editing files, save as, moving tool, bubble tool
10. Design It Yourself!	6–8	architecture, office, business card, introduction to charts, floor plan	creative thinking, sequence and order	texture, square tool, straight line tool, stamp
11. Ancient Egypt	7–10	history, cultures, exhibits, maps, legend, following clues	look up facts, take notes, prepare vocabulary list, encyclopedia, three dimensions	drawing tools, straight line, circle, shade, shadow
12. Tropical Rainforests	7–10	a journey, rainforest ecosystem, facts, plants, animals, letter writing, poster design	binoculars, research skills, maps, percentage, climate, vocabulary building, legend, labels	shade, shadow, texture, outlines, printing to transparency
13. PC Publisher	7–10	a newspaper, magazine, advertisement, headline, comic strips	word processing skills, making an outline, importing graphics, slogans, brainstorm	columns, centering, captions, horizontal line, borders, importing graphics, selecting, saving and retrieving files

SUBJECT INDEX